Blairsville Junior High School
Blairsville, Pennsylvania

The Story of the
INTERNATIONAL
RED CROSS

The Story of the
INTERNATIONAL
RED CROSS

by

Beryl and Sam Epstein

THOMAS NELSON & SONS

Edinburgh   NEW YORK   *Toronto*

Grateful acknowledgment of permission to reproduce photographs is made to: The American Red Cross for pictures on pp. 11, 15 (lower), 49, 61, 62, 69, 75, 76, 77, 79, 87, 91, 92, 99, 156; ATP Bilderdiensi (Zurich) for pictures on pp. 23, 123 (lower); The Australian Red Cross Society, for upper picture on p. 89; Boissonas (Geneva) for pictures on pp. 21, 33 (upper right and lower right), 40, 53 (lower), 65; Philip Boucas for pictures on pp. 15 (upper), 17; The Canadian Red Cross Society for picture at top of p. 157; The French Red Cross Society for the lower picture on p. 157; C. G. George (Geneva) for the pictures on pp. 33 (upper left), 83; The International Committee of the Red Cross for pictures on pp. 21, 23, 33, 37, 38, 40, 53, 65, 66, 80, 81, 83, 85, 105, 106, 108, 112, 119, 123 (upper), 129, 132, 135, 143, 145 (lower), 147, 151, 161, 162, 169, 172; Iugo-Foto (Belgrade) for the picture at the top of p. 145; The League of Red Cross Societies for pictures on pp. 29, 89 (lower), 90, 96, 97, 145 (upper), 149, 152, 157 (lower); Ray Palmer, for pictures on pp. 91, 92; Gerhard Stalling, A. G. (Oldenburg) for picture on p. 135; United Nations for picture on p. 164; World Health Organization for pictures on pp. 15 (upper), 17. *For pictures on the jacket:* Reading clockwise, The American Red Cross, The League of Red Cross Societies, The American Red Cross, and The Australian Red Cross Society.

Third Printing, October 1966

Library of Congress Catalog Card Number: 63–9631

PRINTED IN THE UNITED STATES OF AMERICA

The authors wish to express their thanks for the generous help they received from the International Committee of the Red Cross and the League of Red Cross Societies, both in Geneva, Switzerland, and the Headquarters of the American National Red Cross in Washington, D.C.

Contents

1. "People Helping People"

The story of the International Red Cross might begin in any one of a thousand places where people are helping people. It might begin in the streets of a flooded city, in a land stricken by famine, in a camp crowded with refugees. It might begin in a shell-marked hut where a Red Cross delegate, alone and unarmed, works patiently to persuade opposing military commanders to exchange their wounded prisoners. It might begin a century ago, or today, or any time in between.

It begins, let's say, in the hospital of the Moroccan town of Meknes on the day the first victims of a strange paralyzing disease appear at its door. Eventually that Meknes disease, as it came to be called, would cripple 10,466 Moslem men, women and children, and challenge the Red Cross with a task unique in its history.

Those first patients, all of them from the poorer quarters of Meknes, arrived at the hospital on the morning of September 5, 1959. Some stood holding out hands that had been normal the day before, but which were now useless. Others had been carried to the hospital because they could not walk, and lay helpless near the door. Their feet, in some cases the whole lower part of their bodies, had become paralyzed overnight.

9

The doctors who examined the new arrivals were at first alarmed at what they took to be an outbreak of poliomyelitis. They were even more alarmed when their examinations showed no evidence of polio, or any other known disease. No physician in Meknes could diagnose the tragically crippling ailment. A telephone call to Switzerland brought experts to Meknes by air from the World Health Organization. Even those experts were baffled. While they set in motion an exhaustive search for clues to the mysterious disease, the patients continued to pour in.

By the 10th of September, five days after the first cases had appeared, similar cases were being reported in nearby towns and the Moroccan capital of Rabat, some hundred miles away on the coast. By September 12th the number of new victims each day had risen to two hundred.

The skillful medical detectives of WHO worked for a month before they were able to learn that the disease had been caused by a brownish liquid with which the victims had prepared their food. In actual fact, it was a mixture of cooking oil and a machine oil, manufactured for use in cleaning engines and containing a powerful poison. Unscrupulous dealers had acquired the cheap machine oil in large quantities, flavored it slightly with the oil Moslems normally use, and sold it at bargain rates under a "cooking oil" label.

The Meknes disease permanently destroyed the motor nerves it attacked. Experts agreed that its paralyzed victims could never have their nerves restored; their only hope lay in regular, repeated treatment by therapists able to "teach" healthy muscles to take over the work the paralyzed muscles could no longer perform.

In Morocco itself the number of people trained to do such work could be counted on the fingers of one hand, yet dozens of experts in this highly specialized field were now needed. Morocco also lacked hospital beds, blankets and other equipment to meet an emergency of such vast proportions. Through

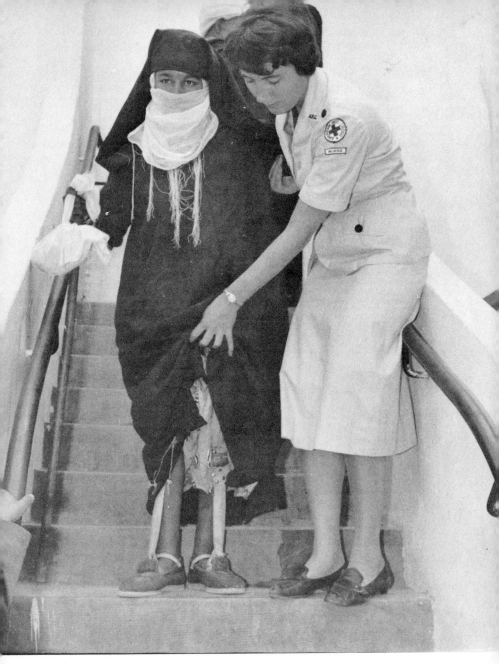

A nurse helps a victim of Meknes disease at the medical center

her own National Society of the Red Cross, known to Moroc-
cans as the Red Crescent Society, Morocco sought help from
the International Red Cross.

The appeal reached Red Cross headquarters in Geneva,
Switzerland, on Tuesday, November 17th. On Wednesday
medical and administrative experts were discussing it. On
Thursday staff members were conferring by telephone, tele-
graph and cable with Red Cross Societies all over the world.
They were asking for contributions of specific kinds of medical equipment, and for cash with which such equipment
could be bought. They were also seeking doctors, nurses and
physiotherapists of a high degree of training—men and
women who were willing and able to leave their homes and
positions temporarily and volunteer for service in Morocco.
Such people were almost certainly going to be difficult to
find; and the task was further complicated by the fact that
at least the majority of the volunteers should be able to speak
and understand French.

Over that week end, in more than a dozen nations, Red
Cross officials talked to heads of hospitals, medical schools
and health ministries, tracking down some of the few people
in the world who had those qualifications, and learning
whether they could be spared from their important jobs. At
the same time other officials were checking emergency supply
depots, and deciding what equipment was immediately available for shipment to Morocco.

By Monday two Societies had reported back to Geneva.
The Swedish Red Cross could promise the services of several
physiotherapists. The Austrian Red Cross was ready to send
Morocco a fully equipped 100-bed hospital unit, plus 2,000
freshly laundered blankets, 1,500 food trays, and several
washing machines.

Two days later contributions of cash were beginning to arrive. The Swedish society made a second report: it was contributing 500 folding beds, along with their mattresses and

bed linens. The Swiss Red Cross announced that it too could promise the services of at least one doctor, and wished to contribute 1,500 blankets, 3,000 sheets, 3,000 towels and 5,000 nightshirts.

By the next day, exactly one week after the appeal had gone out, two dozen doctors and physiotherapists had been recruited—from Denmark, Great Britain, Norway, Sweden, Switzerland and the United States—and details were being worked out for transporting both personnel and material to Morocco. Shortly afterward the air forces of the United States and the German Federal Republic, in response to requests from the Red Cross of their two countries, agreed to co-operate in a mercy air-lift. It went into operation on November 30th.

That day an American Air Force plane was loaded, at a Vienna airport, with the twelve bulky tons of equipment in Austria's hospital-unit gift. The plane landed at the Rabat airport in Morocco early the next morning, where Red Crescent Society members were on hand to unload it, and Moroccan Army trucks stood ready to carry the beds and other goods inland to Meknes. The following afternoon the first of six German planes reached the same airport, with the first shipment of 400 beds promised by the German Red Cross.

Then two more American planes came in. One had flown to Helsinki to pick up 100 beds contributed by the Finnish Red Cross. The other had picked up a cargo of Swiss-donated sheets and blankets in Zurich.

The Turkish Air Force soon joined the air-lift too, as the quantity of gifts for Morocco rose day by day. The Lebanese Red Cross was giving 450 hospital beds and mattresses. The Societies of the Soviet Union were sending 1,000 blankets, 7,500 tins of condensed milk, and two and a half tons of sugar. There were sets of warm full-length underwear for the hundreds of patients known to be children; their treatment was likely to progress faster if they were kept warm.

In the meantime, in fifteen different countries, doctors, physiotherapists and nurses were making last-minute rounds, handing their patients over to colleagues, and saying good-bye to their families at the very beginning of the winter holiday season. They had obtained leaves of absence, and wound up their affairs with all possible speed. They meant to reach Morocco by the first of the new year, within six weeks after the country had first appealed for help.

By then, too, Morocco's Red Crescent Society and teams of public health workers were cleaning out empty disused buildings—in Meknes and other towns. One had been a garage, one a hangar, one an old Foreign Legion barracks. They had not been designed to serve as hospitals or clinics, but they would have to do. All were big enough to accommodate rows of the new beds that were beginning to arrive, along with boxes and crates of other supplies.

On January 1, 1960, the target date toward which hundreds of people had been aiming their efforts, five centers for the treatment and rehabilitation of Morocco's paralysis victims opened their doors. A sixth would be added later. Only one of the hastily readied buildings had been arranged to serve as a hospital for in-patients. The others were prepared to receive the men, women and children who would be brought in for treatment each day. Some would arrive in ambulances contributed by the French Red Cross, some in trucks especially fitted out for carrying cripples.

The real work began when the first patients arrived. None of it was easy. Members of the Red Cross teams sometimes found it difficult even to communicate with each other, because they came from so many different countries. The team at the Meknes center, for example, had been drawn from Canada, Denmark, Germany and Sweden. And almost none of them could talk directly to their patients, most of whom spoke only Arabic. So from the very beginning, when a doctor sat down to examine and question a patient for the first time,

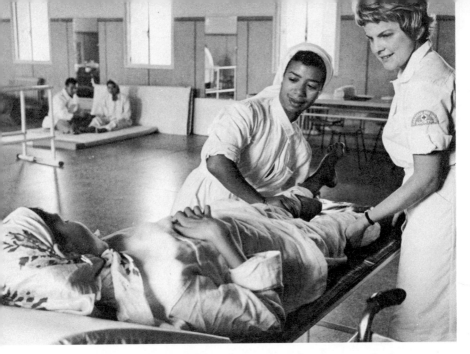

A Canadian physiotherapist and her Moroccan aide treat a patient

An American nurse leads a group of patients in hand exercises

he had to put his queries in French to one of the French-speaking nursing aides Morocco had provided, and the aide had to translate them into Arabic. Then the answers too had to be translated from Arabic back into French again. An examination which had to be long and tedious at best was thus usually even longer and more tedious. But the doctor could not cut it short. His examination was the basis on which each patient's special, individually designed program of treatment was planned.

When the nurses and physiotherapists took over, for long periods of massage and other kinds of physical therapy, they were frustrated too. It was discouraging to exercise a small boy's leg for minutes at a time without being able to say a word to him, or to understand what he was saying.

But a kind of informal language school soon sprang up in every center. An American nurse found herself learning Arabic from her patients, a few words of Swedish perhaps from a fellow nurse, and French medical terms from a team doctor, to augment the school French she used for speaking with her Moroccan aide. It was important that she be able to talk readily with that aide, because one of the functions of the Red Cross teams was to train their Moroccan successors. It was also important that she be able to ask her patients how they felt, and to establish a relationship with them based on respect and trust. She knew she had done a good job when a patient who had been handed on to another nurse, for special treatment, hobbled back to see her a few days later to share with her his excitement about the progress he was making.

The winter was bitterly cold in Morocco that year. Patients arrived at a clinic chilled to the bone after a long ride in an unheated truck. Some of the centers had never received the heating systems promised to the teams. They were icy cold and drafty. Doctors worked in their coats. Nurses put on sweaters beneath their uniforms. Spring brought a welcome warmth.

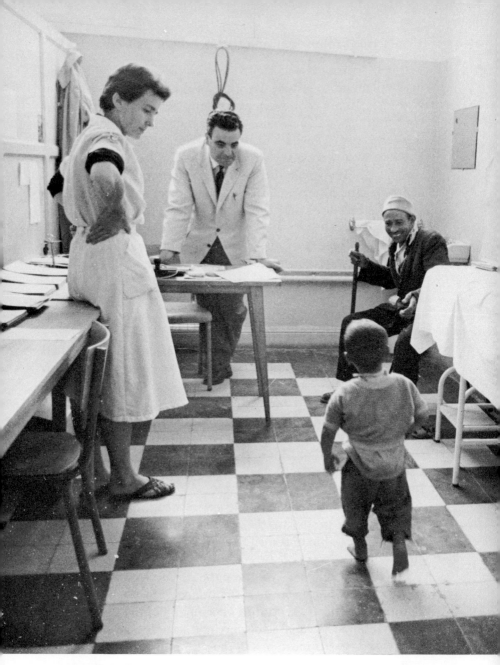

A Swedish physiotherapist and a Belgian doctor give a small patient his final examination

But by spring it was clear that the paralysis project, originally planned to last six months, would have to go on longer than that. Again requests went out from the Geneva office for contributions, and for more doctors, nurses and therapists to replace those who had to return to long-neglected posts at home. The newcomers, like those already doing duty in Morocco, would be given their board and lodging by the Moroccan government. National Red Cross Societies would pay the traveling expenses and the salaries of the men and women they recruited.

By June one out of every five patients, or about 2,000 altogether, no longer needed treatment. Of the 8,500 still being treated, only about three in ten showed much improvement. The task of "teaching" muscles to take on new jobs was a painfully slow one. Many patients would certainly have abandoned the monotonous treatments if they had not had other reasons for coming to the centers day after day. They had found friends there, and they were receiving other than medical help.

Schools had been opened for all the patients less than eighteen years old—half the cripples were in that age group. In their classrooms and recreations rooms they used toys from the cases shipped to Morocco by the Junior Red Cross of the United States, and gift boxes from American and German Juniors.

The adult patients were being given vocational training too, in the hope of preparing them to earn a living again, even if they were not able to return to their former, mostly unskilled, jobs.

By October only a few more patients had been discharged. Plans were made to continue the project into its second year. This time the newly recruited personnel included four orthopedic technicians capable of making the braces and other devices used to support a cripple's muscles and encourage proper movements.

Many of the patients needed such braces temporarily. Some would undoubtedly have to wear supports of some kind all their lives. So the technicians set up a shop in Morocco where they turned out the braces the doctors were prescribing, and where they also taught Moroccan apprentices. Those apprentices would be able to provide orthopedic devices for Moroccan cripples in the future, after the foreigners had returned home.

As the weather turned warm once more, in the spring of 1961, the medical teams' records showed that they had already discharged about 8,000 patients, although nearly 2,000 of that number had to be called back for regular checkups.

The members of the teams began to talk of going home. Their work was coming to an end. One by one they closed down four of the centers. By June 1st only two remained open, and they were being transferred into the capable hands of newly trained Moroccan physiotherapists and their aides, people who from then on would be able to treat polio sufferers and other cripples as well as the remaining victims of the Meknes disease.

The paralysis victims still listed as patients included some 750 who needed only medical supervision from then on, and only 272 who still needed regular treatment. All the rest of that army of more than 10,000 frightened men, women and children had been sent home, most of them fully able to look after themselves and listed as complete "cures."

Newspaper headlines had reported every phase of the project. People all over the world had watched with interest and sympathy the progress the patients made. Doctors were prepared to take advantage of everything the medical team members had learned during their months of work that had no precedent in the annals of medicine.

The Red Cross had made history once more, as it had been making history of one kind or another ever since its founding almost a century before.

2. Henry Dunant, Man with a Vision

The movement known today as the International Red Cross had its beginnings in Switzerland, when a young citizen of Geneva wrote a pamphlet he called *A Memory of Solferino*.

Jean Henri Dunant, who often signed himself Henry Dunant, was not a professional writer. He was a banker and a businessman. He wrote his pamphlet only because he found himself unable to forget what he had seen in the Italian hill town of Solferino a few years earlier.

There, on June 24, 1859, he had watched some 300,000 men fight an all-day battle that left more than 40,000 dead and wounded on the bloodied field of action. There, and in the surrounding countryside in the days that followed, Dunant had watched thousands of those wounded die in agony, their injuries untreated, their most desperate needs ignored.

When he put down on paper what he had seen, he was hoping to arouse in others his own passionate conviction that Europe's wounded soldiers should never again have to endure such hideous suffering, and perish in such numbers from utter neglect. It probably never occurred to him then that someday men and women and children in every part of the globe, during peacetime disasters as well as during wars, would remember him as the founder of a world-wide movement for the relief of human suffering.

Henry Dunant as a young man

Henry Dunant was barely thirty-one in 1859, when he witnessed the battle that changed his own life and the lives of
so many others. Already he had taken an active part in several
humanitarian causes. He had collected food, clothing and
medicine for Geneva's poor and sick. He had made visits to
inmates of the city prison. He had worked with an organization trying to bring about a closer understanding between
Christians and Jews. As a member of a Swiss Young Men's
Christian Union, he had successfully urged the federation of
all similar organizations throughout Europe, and thus helped
found today's international YMCA.

Social welfare work of that kind seemed only natural to
any well-to-do Genevese like Dunant, who took seriously his
obligations as a citizen. It did not interfere with the success
in business that his background and education also fitted him
for. The handsome son of a family deeply rooted in the Geneva of finance and commerce, law and scholarship, he had
entered a bank at the age of twenty-one. At twenty-five he
took over the management of some of the bank's interests in
Algeria. A few years later, ready to go into business for himself, he found other Genevese more than willing to invest in
the various commercial enterprises he undertook.

One of those enterprises brought him to the neighborhood
of Solferino early in the summer of 1859. He had gone to
northern Italy because that was where he hoped to find Napoleon III, Emperor of France and ambitious nephew of Napoleon Bonaparte. Dunant needed the Emperor's authorization
before he could carry out a plan to import windmills into
what was then the French colony of Algeria.

Dunant knew that Napoleon III and his ally, the King of
Sardinia, were engaged in a military campaign to pry loose
Austria's grip on northern Italy. A recent victory had given
them possession of Milan. Now they were moving their forces
into position for the next engagement. But since columns of
marching men move slowly—and armies traveled on foot in

those days—Dunant believed he would have time to interview the Emperor before Napoleon was once more leading his forces into battle.

On the evening of June 23rd Dunant reached the town of Castiglione, having heard that the French headquarters were not far away. There he went to bed in an inn, unaware that Napoleon's men were at that very moment approaching neighboring Solferino, where they would meet advance units of the Austrian army. At three o'clock the next morning Dunant was awakened by gunfire. The historic battle of Solferino had begun.

For the next fifteen hours Dunant watched the titanic struggle from the vantage of a hill outside Castiglione. At last darkness and a storm put a stop to the fighting. The Austrians withdrew from their battered positions. The thunder of artillery died. But it was not until daybreak that the terrible cost of the battle could even be guessed. It would never

A detail from Carlo Bossoli's painting of the battle of Solferino

be accurately counted. And no adequate medical corps stood ready to save the lives of the thousands of men whose torn flesh was already turning gangrenous under a hot sun.

In 1859 medical corps as they are known today were un-dreamed of. Every army had its doctors, but they were few in number and their aides were usually blundering and inex-perienced. The reason for such inadequacy was that the thinking of military leaders had not yet caught up with the vast changes that had taken place in patterns of warfare dur-ing the previous century.

Before the French Revolution European armies had been for the most part fairly small forces of professional soldiers. That conflict, and the Napoleonic wars that followed, had introduced the use of huge numbers of fighting men, many of them untrained volunteers and hastily drafted conscripts. And these new "people's armies" had new kinds of artillery, far greater in range and power than any that had been known before. But the small haphazardly organized medical corps of an earlier day had scarcely changed at all.

It is hardly surprising that nineteenth-century warfare seemed unbelievably horrible to those who had been brought up on stories of the "glory" of war—and to Henry Dunant, who had been brought up to believe that it was his duty to relieve suffering wherever he saw it.

That morning, after the battle of Solferino, the quarter-master corps of the French army was assigned the task of collecting the wounded and carrying them to the inadequate shelters designated as field hospitals. There a handful of army surgeons did their best to bandage some of the worst wounds, sew up gaping flesh, and amputate shattered limbs. After-ward the casualties were carried to the nearest villages. There some were laid on the straw-covered floors of churches, town halls, schools and private houses, until all such space was filled. Others, by the hundreds, many among them already dying, were simply put down among swarms of flies, under the blazing sun, in courtyards, public streets and squares.

Dunant was still in Castiglione that morning when the first wounded were brought in. When he saw that no one remained to look after them, and that there was no hope of moving them to the neighborhood's overflowing hospitals, he hastily called on the village women to help him do for the soldiers what little could be done.

Hour after hour, for days, he worked among the injured. "The gentleman in white," soldiers called him, as he knelt in the dust in his linen suit, bathing festering wounds, offering sips of water, filling pipes with the tobacco he sent his coachman to nearby Brescia to buy.

Finally, exhausted by his heartbreaking ordeal, Dunant left Italy.

He could not leave behind him the knowledge of how little help had been given to those men in agonizing need.

As the months went by he found himself obsessed with the idea of doing something—he didn't yet know what—to alleviate the sufferings of other soldiers in the future.

Simply to talk against war itself did not strike him as enough. His own country, pledged to "perpetual neutrality," seemed unlikely ever again to be involved in conflict with another nation. The brief civil war its people had fought, when Dunant himself was in his teens, had confirmed the widespread Swiss belief in the futility of all war. Yet Dunant knew, as he later wrote, that "no man can say with certainty that he is forever safe from the possibility of war." And even if no Swiss ever fell in battle again, men of other nationalities were almost certain to do so. It was for them that he was so deeply concerned. He felt that all wounded men deserved the best care their fellow human beings could provide.

But how could that care be brought to them immediately after they were injured, when they needed it most, when there was still a chance that their lives could be saved? That was the question he found himself trying to answer.

Dunant was neither ignorant nor naive. He knew he was not the first man to desire some improvement in the care of the wounded.

A few years earlier, when British forces were fighting Russians in the Crimea, the world's first war correspondent, William Russell, had written angry dispatches to the London *Times.*

"Not only are there not sufficient surgeons . . ." Russell had declared, "not only are there no dressers and nurses . . . there is not even linen to make bandages."

The response to those dispatches had been shocked disbelief on the part of many readers who still thought of a battlefield as a stage for heroic drama. Yet they had produced their effect. One of England's first real trained nurses, Florence Nightingale, organized a small group of women and took it to the Crimea under government auspices. "I do not mean that I believe the *Times* accounts," she had explained to a friend before she left, "but I do believe we may be of use to the poor wounded wretches."

The Grand Duchess Helena Pavlovna and a group of Russian nurses also went to the Crimea to care for their own wounded. And thousands of generous-minded people in various lands, once they became convinced of the many unfilled needs of wounded soldiers, collected large quantities of bandages, lint and other medical necessities of the day and forwarded them to the battle fronts.

But thousands had died in the Crimea before the first nurses reached there. Other thousands died afterward, because they were not brought soon enough to the hospitals the nurses staffed and the public's offerings helped to equip. Yet no country, so far as Dunant knew, had profited by such examples to set up an effective system for caring for its injured soldiers from the very beginning of a conflict, from the moment a war's first shot had been fired.

Then he recalled a remark made by a woman of Geneva

at the time Napoleon III and the King of Sardinia were beginning to marshal their troops against Austria. She had suggested that a committee of Genevese women should start
immediately to prepare dressings for the wounds the soldiers
on both sides were bound to suffer.

Dunant himself had been among the many who persuaded
her to abandon a scheme they called premature.

"How can you think of making dressings before a single
man has been wounded?" he had asked her.

Now, haunted by his memory of those dying men at Solferino, he wondered how many of them might have been
saved if that woman's suggestion had been acted upon.

Suddenly he was able to visualize the outlines of the plan
he had been searching for. In order to present it to the public
in such a way that it too would not be scorned, he sat down to
write *A Memory of Solferino*.

Most of the book was a description of what he had seen
during those unforgettable days in Italy.

He wrote first of the battle itself, and every word reflected
the horror he had felt on that hilltop.

He described "Austrians and Allies trampling each other
underfoot, killing one another on piles of bleeding corpses,
felling their enemies with their rifle butts, crushing skulls,
ripping bellies open with saber and bayonet. No quarter is
given; it is sheer butchery; a struggle between savage beasts,
maddened with blood and fury . . .

"Here comes the artillery," he wrote, as if he were seeing
it all again in that very moment. "The guns crash over the
dead and the wounded, strewn pell-mell on the ground.
Brains spurt under the wheels, limbs are broken and torn,
bodies mutilated past recognition—the soil is literally puddled
with blood, and the plain littered with human remains."

Then he took up the aftermath of the battle. He told how
soldiers were detailed to identify and bury the dead, many of
whom "lay hidden in ditches, in trenches, or concealed under

bushes or mounds of earth," so that they were not found for some time and "gave forth a fearful stench." Haste and carelessness and negligence, he thought, had caused "more than one living man" to be buried with the dead in the large common grave.

He described the fate of the injured who had been carried off the field and brought in to Castiglione and the other villages, where they lay hungry, thirsty, and in pain, their wounds unbandaged, their bodies verminous.

"With faces black with flies that swarmed around their wounds," Dunant wrote, "men gazed around them, wild-eyed and helpless. . . . There was one poor man, completely disfigured, with a broken jaw and his swollen tongue hanging out of his mouth. He was tossing and trying to get up. I moistened his dry lips and hardened tongue. . . . Another wretched man had a part of his face—nose, lips and chin—taken off with a saber cut. He could not speak, and lay, half-blind, making heart-rending signs with his hands and uttering guttural sounds to attract attention. . . . A third, with his skull gaping wide open, was dying, spitting out his brains on the stone floor . . ."

Dunant explained that the Italian women he had called on to help him had at first aided only the French and Sardinian soldiers, because they thought of them as friends who had come to northern Italy to rescue them from a hated Austrian domination. The Austrian wounded, who had also been carried into Castiglione, were despised and therefore ignored.

But when the women saw that Dunant himself treated all the men alike—though he felt special sympathy for the Austrians because they were "forced to suffer not only physical pain, but also the griefs of captivity"—the villagers were quick to follow his example. *Tutti fratelli,* Dunant heard the women saying to each other from then on. "All are brothers."

"All honor to these compassionate women, to these girls of Castiglione!" Dunant wrote.

Red Cross Juniors plant a cypress in Solferino on the centenary of the battle

His admiration of them, however, had not blinded him to their limitations. Because most of them were "untrained or injudicious," as he put it, they often tried to feed a man food he was too weak or sick to take.

Dunant also added that "At the end of a week, or ten days, the charitable zeal of the people . . . sincere as it was, began to cool off . . . volunteers withdrew one by one, for they could no longer bear to look upon suffering they could do so little to relieve."

"Oh, how valuable it would have been in those Lombardy towns," Dunant wrote, "to have had a hundred experienced and qualified voluntary orderlies and nurses! Such a group would have formed a nucleus around which could have been rallied the help . . . which needed competent guidance. As it was, there was no time for those who knew their business to give the needful advice and guidance, and most of those who brought their own goodwill to the task lacked the necessary knowledge and experience, so that their efforts were inadequate and often ineffective . . ."

He was reaching the point of the message he had chosen to introduce so dramatically.

"But why have I told you of all these scenes of pain and distress . . .?" he asked near the end of the pamphlet. "Why have I lingered with seeming complacency over lamentable pictures, tracing their details with what may appear desperate fidelity?

"It is a natural question. Perhaps I might answer it by another:

"Would it not be possible, in time of peace and quiet, to form relief societies for the purpose of having care given to the wounded in wartime by zealous, devoted and thoroughly qualified volunteers?"

A Memory of Solferino, with its pointed question about relief societies to be formed "in time of peace and quiet," was published in November 1862. Less than two years later that question had its answer, and the phrase, "the red cross," had entered the language of mankind.

3. The Red Cross Is Born

The moment Dunant's little book was off the press, he began distributing copies of it at his own expense to every part of Europe where he thought it might be read sympathetically.

He was heartened by the response.

Kings and queens, royal princes and princesses, prime ministers and generals, doctors, lawyers and writers in every part of the continent—almost all who read Dunant's ugly words about war and the ravages of war—recognized them as true. When they came to his suggestion for a means of alleviating the agony of war's victims, many declared it was practical and workable, and deserved the most serious considerations. Certain military leaders particularly praised it as a solution to one of their most serious problems.

Not everyone applauded his idea. There were military men among its opponents. They objected to the very thought of civilians having a hand in what they regarded as exclusively military matters.

To Dunant's surprise and dismay, Florence Nightingale also refused to support his plan. She said that British authorities had at last set up an organization capable of caring for their wounded in wartime—and that in any case all such work should be left to governments. If volunteers accepted responsibility for this heavy burden, she pointed out, they would in effect be offering to share the costs of war; and this, she felt, would encourage governments to go to war more often. Other people agreed with her.

In every capital of Europe Dunant's book stirred up discussion. His ideas fitted in with other fairly new ones which had crossed the Atlantic after the American Revolution and helped set off the great Revolution in France. Even Napoleon Bonaparte, finding himself surrounded by thousands of corpses and "countless wounded men," after the terrible battle of Marengo half a century earlier, had written his enemy, the Emperor of Austria, imploring him "to listen to the voice of humanity." But Bonaparte himself had continued to plan the strategy of each battle far more carefully than he planned the care of those it would inevitably injure. And many men of Dunant's own day still found it easier to talk of humanity than to join in any permanent program for the assistance of individual human beings.

It was only in Geneva that Dunant's book actually roused men to immediate action.

Early in February of 1863, just three months after the book's publication, it was the subject of debate at a regular meeting of the distinguished group of philanthropists known as the Public Welfare Society. The result was a decision to form a committee to promote Dunant's ideas.

The prominent lawyer, Gustave Moynier, who was the Society's president and a man of remarkable organizing ability, agreed to serve on the committee himself. So did aristocratic General Guillaume Dufour, who had led the Swiss federal forces during the country's last war, and who had then told his officers that "when you drive the enemy back, look after their wounded as you would our own and accord them all the respect which is due their misfortune."

Two other members were doctors of medicine, Theodore Maunoir and Louis Appia. Dr. Appia had taken charge of

Dr. Theodore Maunoir

Dr. Louis Appia

Gustave Moynier

General G. H. Dufour

the shipments of lint and bandages which went out from Geneva as soon as word had reached the city of the desperate need after the battle of Solferino. He had always, in fact, interested himself in practical care for the wounded, and was the designer of a light simple vehicle for transporting injured men from battlefield to hospital.

Henry Dunant himself, although never a member of the Welfare Society, was asked to be the fifth member of what came to be known as the Committee of Five.

In mid-February the Committee held its first meeting. Earnestly and in detail Dunant outlined his plan to the other four men, all of them except Appia considerably older and more experienced than himself.

The first objective, he declared, should be to establish in each country voluntary "medical societies" for the relief of the wounded in time of war. The societies should be set up immediately, he said—not at some time when an individual country found itself on the verge of a conflict. They should be approved, or recognized in some way by their governments, so that their work on a battlefield would have the protection of military authorities. And they should remain in permanent existence, "their activities inspired by a real spirit of international charity." Each society, in other words, should stand ready to aid the injured of every land, whenever and wherever its help might be needed.

The Committee members soon decided to set in motion an ambitious scheme. They planned to invite representatives of other nations to meet in a conference with them, to discuss Dunant's proposals.

It was an astonishingly bold decision for any five men to make, especially as they did not fully agree among themselves. Two important points of difference had come up almost immediately between Dunant and Moynier, the lawyer.

Moynier thought the duty of each society should be to care solely for the wounded men of its own nationality. Dunant visualized a wider role for each society, in a framework of what he called "neutrality."

Dunant was using the word "neutrality," in that connection, to mean "immune from harm." He thought, for example, that every soldier, once he had been wounded, should be regarded as a "neutral." An injured man, Dunant argued, who could no longer fight, was no longer a combatant; as a noncombatant, he deserved to be regarded simply as a human being in need of help. And that help, Dunant believed, should be given to him freely by the first trained person who saw his need, whether that person was connected with the wounded man's own army, or with the opposing force.

Members of relief societies should also, Dunant said, be treated as neutrals when they volunteered their services during a war. They too would be noncombatants, taking neither side in a conflict. They would be on the battlefield only to aid the wounded. Thus they too should be immune to harm from the soldiers of both belligerents.

On this particular point Dunant eventually had his way. The principle of neutrality he stood for became vital to all the work of the International Red Cross.

Moynier almost immediately won the other basic argument. It too had to do with neutrality, though in the word's more usual sense of political neutrality on a national level. That argument arose out of the fact that Dunant wanted Paris to be the center from which relief societies would be organized. Paris, he said, was the capital toward which most Europeans looked for everything that was new and advanced. From Paris had sprung the humanitarian ideals that had been sweeping through Europe since the time of the French Revolution: therefore Paris should be the home of the societies he saw as Europe's first true adventure in international humanitarianism.

Moynier wanted Geneva, not Paris, to be the societies' home. He said that the French Revolution itself, and its forerunner the American Revolution, had both been largely inspired by the writings of Jean Jacques Rousseau—and that Rousseau had been born in Geneva. But Geneva also had an even better claim, Moynier believed, simply because it was a Swiss city. Only a neutral nation—a nation pledged not to take sides in any future war—could be the natural home of the kind of societies they were discussing. If such societies were sponsored in Paris, he was convinced, every foe of France would regard them as somehow French in spirit, and consequently worthless. Sponsored by Switzerland, who had no enemies, and whose political neutrality had long been recognized by other nations, the societies would arouse no such antagonism.

The rest of the Committee agreed with Moynier. Dunant was overruled. The international leaders who were asked to meet with the Committee of Five, in October of that same year, were invited to assemble in Geneva.

Before that meeting took place, during the spring and summer of 1863, Dunant himself traveled from one European city to another, talking with brilliant persuasiveness wherever he went about the subject that now absorbed his full attention. He appeared at a statistical congress in Berlin, because it would give him the opportunity to talk with men of several countries—and he won many converts there.

He visited the small states that would eventually be united into Germany, and in almost every one he was received by someone of great authority. In Saxony the King gave Dunant an audience. In Prussia the King's brother listened attentively when Dunant spoke, and introduced him to the chief medical officers of the Prussian army. In Austria a grand duke received Dunant on the Emperor's behalf. Napoleon III let it be known that he approved Dunant's ideas.

Even so Dunant and the other members of the Committee were amazed when fifteen separate states or nations sent delegates to Geneva for an informal discussion on "putting

Monsieur Dunant's suggestions into operation." There were government officials, lawyers and doctors in the group. They came from Austria, France, Great Britain, and Italy; from the Netherlands, Russia, Spain, and Sweden, and from Prussia and six smaller German states.

For four days the distinguished guests and their Swiss hosts talked together. They proved to be of one mind. All present agreed that governments should encourage the creation of private societies of volunteers trained to aid the wounded in time of war. Each society should be linked to the medical service of its own national army. And the various societies should be ready to assist each other in time of need. The Committee of Five would develop and maintain the relationships among them.

Dr. Appia also suggested that all those aiding the wounded at the front should wear a distinguishing mark, such as a white arm band, as a signal that they were neutral noncombatants deserving protection. Someone pointed out that a white arm band might not always be readily visible in the smoke and confusion of battle.

The arm band worn by Dr. Appia in three wars

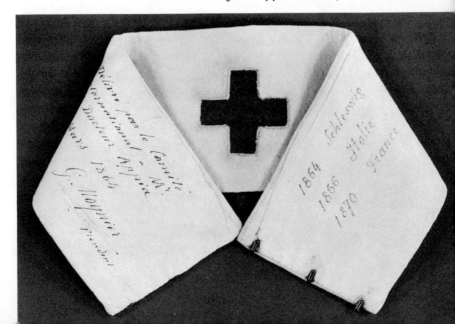

Then someone else—most accounts say it was the Swiss General Dufour—suggested that a bright red cross in the center of the white band would make it more noticeable. The design of a red cross on a white field is the reverse of the Swiss flag, which bears a white cross on a field of red. Perhaps that is why the rest of the delegates accepted the new idea immediately. Perhaps it was their way of honoring the Swiss gentlemen who had called them together. In any case, the symbol that has now become famous as the sign of the Red Cross was decided upon before that meeting ended on October 30, 1863.

The first national relief society came into existence two months later in the little German kingdom of Württemberg. Within a few weeks the small Duchy of Oldenburg and the powerful state of Prussia also had such societies. The December issue of the popular French magazine, *L'Illustration*, carried an artist's salute to Dunant's plan. It was a sketch of "the battlefield of the future," showing civilian volunteers, wearing white arm bands marked with red crosses, caring for wounded men under fire.

An artist's salute to the Red Cross in L'Illustration *for December, 1863*

About a month later Dr. Appia put on a little hand-sewn white arm band, to which a cross of red cloth had been stitched, and wore it onto a real battlefield. On February 1, 1864, war had been declared between Prussia and Denmark, and the five-man Geneva Committee had immediately sent him to the front to aid the injured.

Appia was acquainted with several Prussian army doctors and officers. They knew his skill and his experience with battle injuries. They also knew him as a citizen of neutral Switzerland, which had no stake in the Danish-Prussian quarrel. They gave him complete freedom to go where he wished, and issued orders for his protection.

Members of the pioneer relief societies recently organized in Württemberg, Oldenburg and Prussia soon tried to join Appia at the front. They were turned back before they could reach him. Army commanders on both sides mistrusted the volunteers, perhaps as possible spies hiding behind the sign of the red cross, perhaps merely as civilian amateurs who had no place on a battlefield. None of the volunteers was permitted to carry out the work he had come to do until Appia interceded on his behalf.

Appia returned to Geneva, when the brief war was over, with the report that a red cross arm band was not the protection they had all hoped it would be. It did not serve as a passport for reaching the wounded on the field. A military commander seemed willing to honor the symbol only when, as in Appia's case, he happened to know the wearer and trusted him personally. And no civilian could argue against an officer's decision. A military commander was answerable only to the government he served.

It was a discouraging report. There seemed to be little point in organizing relief societies if they were not going to be permitted to fulfill their purpose. But how could they be guaranteed the right to carry out their life-saving work unless military authorities were compelled to accept their services?

And how could that be accomplished unless governments themselves—kings and queens and legislatures—issued orders to that effect to their military commanders?

The Geneva Committee decided to try to bring about an agreement among governments to issue such orders.

Their decision was a great deal more startling in 1864 than it might be today. The kind of agreement the men of Geneva were thinking of had never been achieved up to that time.

Two or more governments had, of course, often agreed to the terms of a peace treaty or a defense alliance. A dozen years earlier France had even invited eleven other nations to join her in accepting quarantine regulations designed to prevent the spread of epidemics, although only two governments were willing to accept the idea. But a permanent international agreement, of a purely humanitarian nature, had never even been proposed to the nations of the world.

The signing of the First Geneva Convention

Furthermore the members of the Geneva Committee, as ordinary citizens, could make no proposals at all, even to a single government. Only another government could do that. Nevertheless they were determined to go ahead with their plan. First they wrote out a draft of the kind of agreement they hoped might be reached. Surprisingly enough—or so it seems today—the draft made no mention at all of relief societies.

Moynier and General Dufour agreed that its chief purpose must be the protection of the wounded, and protection of those who cared for them, whether they were military doctors or volunteer civilians. Although Moynier and Dufour might approve Dunant's ideas about permanent cilivilan relief societies, they knew such societies would not immediately be welcomed by all governments and all military authorities.

But even a government not willing to encourage the formation of a relief society might still be willing to guarantee protection of the wounded and of those—whoever they might be—who cared for them. And if every government would agree to that, a great deal would have been achieved.

The Geneva Committee members then approached the Swiss government, to ask it to invite other governments to join in a diplomatic conference in Geneva. The Committee members were prominent and influential men, well known to the Swiss political party leaders then in power. Their request was granted.

And so it came about that invitations to a history-making conference went out to all the principal countries of Europe and to Brazil, Mexico and the United States. The conference was to open on August 8, 1864. Moynier would attend as an official delegate of the Swiss government. The other members of the Committee, having no diplomatic standing, would not even be able to address the conference, although it was understood that they would be admitted as unofficial guests.

Many of the governments which had received the invitation replied with gratifying speed. On the appointed date the expected delegates arrived and met in Geneva's handsome Town Hall.

Most of the states and nations which had sent unofficial delegates to the meeting the year before sent official diplomats now. Among the few exceptions were the Catholic states of Austria and Bavaria; both had decided to ignore a movement originating in the Protestant stronghold of Geneva. But Belgium, Portugal and Denmark, which had shown no interest in the previous meeting, sent delegates to this one. And there were two Americans present, Abraham Lincoln's minister to Switzerland and a doctor named Charles S. Bowles.

Both Americans were warmly welcomed. They seemed to offer proof that what had begun as a purely European movement was already drawing attention and support in the New World. They were valued for another reason too. They could answer questions about President Lincoln's own pioneering attempt to bring compassion to the field of battle. That attempt had taken the form of *Instructions for the conduct of the United States Army in the field,* issued at the beginning of the Civil War which was then still in progress. Those *Instructions* provided for the best possible care of the wounded of both sides, and for the humane treatment of prisoners of war. The Geneva Committee had found them a useful guide when it prepared its draft agreement for the diplomats' consideration.

Dr. Bowles, one of the Americans, could also have provided information about an organization he worked with, an organization that closely resembled the relief societies Dunant believed in. Originally a group of women volunteers ready to prepare bandages and nurse the wounded, it had been transformed into a government-authorized Sanitary Commission when the Union Army's medical service proved unable to cope with the thousands of Civil War casualties. Prominent people in all walks of life, both men and women, had given their services to the Commission. With government backing, and wide popular support, it had accomplished a great deal. The hospitals it staffed and equipped were considered especially fine.

Dunant himself would have been glad if the diplomats meeting in Geneva had studied the American Sanitary Commission. But all official discussions were limited strictly to the points in the draft agreement prepared by the Geneva Committee. The conference lasted for two weeks. At the end of that time the delegates had voted to approve ten specific points, or articles. The most important were these:

That all medical personnel active at the front or behind the lines during wartime—this included members of army medical corps and any volunteers permitted to work with them—should be regarded as "neutrals"; that is, they should be immune to harm from either side. The same protection was also to be given to clergymen.

That all military hospitals and ambulance wagons should also be regarded as "neutral," and therefore deserving of protection.

That a red cross on a white field should symbolize "neutrality" and guarantee protection not only to the wounded and those who cared for them, but also to hospitals, ambulances and other medical equipment.

That captured medical personnel should be allowed either to look after the wounded held by their captors, or be returned to their own forces.

That all wounded men must be treated alike, and that wounded prisoners should be exchanged whenever possible.

All the articles, together, were called *La Convention de Genève*. The French name—French was then the accepted language of diplomacy—meant simply "The Geneva Agreement" or "The Geneva Treaty." It has usually been translated into English, however, as the Geneva Convention, and this has proved confusing to those who think of a convention as a conference, or a meeting. So it is a point to remember that the words Geneva Convention, which appear so often in the story of the Red Cross, never refer to a coming-together of people; instead they always mean the coming-together of minds in an agreement.

The Geneva Convention was left "open." That is, all nations were free to agree to it whether they had been represented at the conference or not.

Some of the delegates had been given the authority to sign any agreement that was reached on behalf of their governments. Others had to return home and obtain their governments' permission before they signed. But no signature, by itself, bound any country to the agreement. That could be done only by ratification. Each government, in other words, had to make the agreement part of the actual law of its own land, by whatever process was customary. In some cases a king's decree transformed the agreement into law. In others— in republican Switzerland, for example—the vote of the legislature was necessary.

France was the first to ratify the Geneva Convention, on September 22, 1864, just a month after the conference ended. Nine other nations followed in swift succession before that year was out—Switzerland and Belgium in October; the Netherlands in November; Italy, Sweden, Norway, Spain, Denmark and the small Duchy of Baden all in December.

The next year five more countries ratified: Greece, Great Britain, Prussia, Turkey and little Mecklenburg-Schwerin. The year afterward there were six more: Austria, Portugal and four small German states.

Catholic Austria's sudden decision to join the Convention was reached as a result of the Austro-Prussian War, which occurred that year. Prussia's newly formed Society for Relief to Wounded Soldiers had gone into immediate action as soon as the fighting began. Its members organized seventy hospital trains and mobilized nearly 2,000 volunteers, 800 of them nurses, to care for the injured of both sides. The practical advantages of this humanitarianism so impressed the Austrian rulers that they abandoned their mistrust of a Protestant-inspired agreement, and signed the Convention before the war was over. A few years later the Convention was also ratified by the Holy See, the Italian territory then ruled by the Pope; from that time on no Catholic nation held out against it on religious grounds.

Turkey's signature had special significance. That Moslem nation had for centuries regarded all Christian lands as her enemies. Now, her once-vast empire shrunk, she had become economically dependent on Europe and was eager for friends there. Her government, the Sublime Porte, agreed to the Convention chiefly to cement relations with the European nations that had already joined it. But this act brought the first non-Christian country into the movement Dunant had started, and established its essentially nonreligious character for all time.

The Geneva Convention was unique. It represented man's first effort to create a permanent body of international humanitarian law. It opened up vast new possibilities for a better future for mankind. It could not guarantee that future.

In other words this new instrument—this historic experiment—might remain nothing more than an interesting piece of parchment in the Swiss archives. It could be enforced on a national level, of course. Once a nation had ratified it, had made the Convention part of its own national law, that nation could hold its own military authorities responsible for obeying it. It could legally punish a military commander, for example, for refusing to protect the wounded of his own or an enemy's army.

But what authority could punish a nation which refused to obey the Convention?

There was no such authority. This new international law could not be enforced on an international level.

The five Genevese who had brought the Convention into being had achieved their original goal. They had seen their own humanitarian ideals become the ideals—on paper, at least—of most of the governments of Europe. But now those men realized that they could not simply disband, their place in history already secure. They realized that it was up to them, because there was no one else to take the responsibility, to see to it that those ideals were put into practice.

They had no power to bring a government into line if it chose to ignore the agreement it had signed. But they believed they could arouse public opinion in favor of the Convention, so that any government which ignored its principles would have to bear the weight of public disapproval. They set themselves to do that in two ways.

They continued to send their own delegates onto battlefields, to learn at first hand whether or not the regulations of the Convention were being followed. A delegate's factual report told the belligerents of both sides how well the military commanders were observing the terms of the Convention. Each government at war could then take whatever action it chose, or deemed necessary, to prove itself humanitarian even in time of war.

The Committee of Five, eventually known as the International Committee of the Red Cross—the ICRC, also worked steadily for the creation of relief societies that were soon calling themselves Red Cross Societies. And those Societies, linked together by the ICRC, could muster considerable public support in favor of the Convention's principles.

Some of the Societies met opposition from military authorities who did not openly flout the Convention, but who chose to ignore the organizations' offer of aid for the wounded. When such commanders needed volunteer helpers to care for injured soldiers, they preferred to bestow red cross arm bands on individual civilians from villages nearby. Those civilians might be as untrained for the task as the women of Castiglione whose help Dunant had sought; but they could be dismissed and forgotten the moment they were no longer needed. They didn't belong to a Society that took on responsibilities which—according to those military authorities—it had no right to assume.

But some military men did recognize the value of trained and organized relief societies. And one government after another authorized its own national Society to serve as the volunteer arm of its military medical corps in time of war. This happened most readily in countries where the Societies were headed by important public figures. Many were. The Grand Duchess of Baden, for example, led the Society organized in the Duchy of Baden.

By the year 1869, ten years after the battle of Solferino, Dunant's ideas had given birth to many Red Cross Societies, and to a Geneva Convention already signed—and generally respected—by twenty-two nations. Within a single decade Henry Dunant and the four other members of the Geneva Committee had lifted to a new level the conscience of a whole continent.

4. The Woman Who Dared to Act

When the Red Cross was ten years old it was still a purely European movement. It had taken no roots in any other continent.

To the members of the Geneva Committee this was both disappointing and puzzling, particularly so far as the United States was concerned. The Geneva Convention owed a good deal to those *Instructions* Lincoln had issued to his troops. The program of the American voluntary Sanitary Commission had been a useful guide for Red Cross Societies' activities. And since the close of the Civil War Americans had paid great honor to a brave woman who had gone onto some of the worst of that war's battlefields, to care for the wounded. To Red Cross members that woman—her name was Clara Barton—seemed a perfect illustration of the kind of work their Societies had been formed to do. Yet the United States still had no Red Cross Society of its own, and had twice ignored opportunities to sign the Geneva Convention.

The first of these opportunities had occurred at the diplomatic meeting in Geneva in 1864, when two Americans had been among the delegates. Present as observers only, they had nevertheless promised to try to persuade their government to join the Convention. Their efforts had been completely unsuccessful.

Clara Barton

The second opportunity came not long after the end of the American Civil War. Dr. Henry Bellows, who had served as chief of the Sanitary Commission, urged his government to sign the Convention. He and other former Sanitary Commission members had even formed an organization to promote the idea. But he too failed in his purpose, and the organization disbanded.

One day in the autumn of 1869 the members of the Geneva Committee learned that Clara Barton was in Switzerland, visiting their own city. They determined to call on her. They knew she had come to Europe for her health—that she had been exhausted by her years of war work, and the months she had spent afterward trying to trace the thousands of soldiers who had been reported missing at the war's end. But they took it for granted that she approved of the Red Cross and would be willing to talk about it with them. They were encouraged by her cordial welcome when they presented themselves.

"We wish to learn, if possible," one of the Committee told her, "why your country has declined to sign the Geneva Convention. We know America is a generous and humanitarian nation. Her position is incomprehensible to us."

"Just what does America object to?" another Committee member asked. "And how could her objections be overcome?"

The small middle-aged woman listened to them silently, as if she were puzzled. "I have never in America heard of the Geneva Convention," she said finally.

They were astounded. They knew she had been ill at the time Dr. Bellows had made his efforts on the Convention's behalf. But she would almost certainly have heard of it even so, if his efforts had aroused any public interest at all. The Swiss visitors had to accept the probability that most Americans shared Clara Barton's ignorance of the work to which they had given ten years.

Now, however, Clara Barton seemed eager to learn about

their organization and its achievement. The talk they had with her that day set off a chain of events that not only brought the United States into the Geneva Convention and the Red Cross movement, but gave the Red Cross itself a new direction and a wider scope.

Neither result occurred quickly. But while Clara Barton remained in Switzerland, at her doctor's orders, she became actively involved with the European Red Cross. Three days after war broke out between Prussia and France, in July 1870, Dr. Appia called on her again. This time he and the men with him were on their way to the front. He invited her to join them, to do the kind of work she had already done in her own country.

"No shot had been fired—no man had fallen," Clara Barton wrote later. "Yet this organized, powerful commission was on its way, with its skilled agents, ready to receive, direct and dispense the charities and accumulations which the generous sympathies of twenty-two nations, if applied to, might place at its disposal. These men had treaty power to go directly on to any field, and work unmolested . . . their supplies held sacred and their efforts recognized and seconded in every direction by either belligerent army."

She had often felt, especially during the early part of the American Civil War, that the Sanitary Commission's well-meaning volunteers were insufficiently prepared for the task they had taken on, and that they seldom got close enough to the front lines to give injured men the very help they needed most. When she had gone into the front lines herself it was as an individual, not as a member of the Commission, and often she had to argue her way past officers unwilling to allow a civilian on the field. Now she recognized the Swiss Red Cross group as uniquely prepared to prevent the kind of tragedies she had witnessed at Fredericksburg, Virgina, for example. There she had seen, as she put it, "starving wounded, frozen to the ground," lying neglected and uncared for because the Sanitary Commission and its supplies were still in Washington, "with no effective organization to get beyond." Such memories made her eager to see how Appia's organization functioned.

She refused his invitation because, she said, she feared her own lack of strength would hamper his group's efforts. But a week later she set out on her own. She had found—as so often happened during her long life—the new strength she needed in order to do what she wanted to do. She went first to Basel, where the International Red Cross Committee had opened a central supply headquarters for its war relief program. Most of the volunteers at work there were members of Switzerland's own national Red Cross Society.

The little city on Switzerland's northern border, with France close to one side and Prussia on the other, was fearful of being overrun by one warring force or the other at any moment. But the volunteers were calmly sorting the supplies that would be sent out to hundreds of workers already in the field.

"My first steps were to the storehouses," Clara Barton reported afterward to friends, "and to my amazement I found there a larger supply than I had ever seen at any one time . . . at our own sanitary commission rooms in Washington, even in the fourth year of the war; and the trains were loaded with boxes and barrels pouring in from every city, town and hamlet in Switzerland, even from Austria and Northern Italy; and the trained, educated nurses stood awaiting their appointments, each with this badge upon the arm or breast; and every box, package or barrel with a broad scarlet cross . . ."

Within days she was heading for the front herself, determined to see if those supplies, so efficiently centralized, would be as efficiently used on the Franco-Prussian battlefields. Through Dr. Appia she met the Grand Duchess Louise of Baden, who had turned several of her palaces into Red Cross

The vicar of Meudon protects a burial detail with a Red Cross flag

Red Cross workers care for wounded prisoners of the Franco-Prussian War

hospitals. The head of the Baden Red Cross, daughter of the King of Prussia, and the American woman born in a New England village, immediately became friends. Clara Barton offered her help. The Duchess accepted it.

For some weeks Clara Barton nursed the wounded in a large hospital depot at Karlsruhe, and went out from there to aid the wounded still lying on the field. Then the French city of Strasbourg fell to the Prussians and their German allies, who had been besieging it for weeks, and she was asked to go there.

The Duchess wanted to help the thousands of hungry, needy women, old men and children within the defeated city's walls. Other wealthy German philanthropists were willing to help too. But they could not work through the Red Cross whose program was limited to aiding war wounded. So Clara Barton agreed to undertake, independently, the distribution of their gifts.

Her approach to certain problems amazed her European friends. When the Duchess offered to furnish clothing for the city's poor, Clara Barton asked instead for cash and for material enough for 30,000 garments. They would enable her, she said, to pay Strasbourg women to make up the necessary clothes, "and thus create an industry." The sewing shop she opened on a large flat rock—it was later moved into a roofed workroom—was the first important step toward the city's rehabilitation. It also gave European Red Cross people their first glimpse of a kind of humanitarian service that was new to them.

Clara Barton, for her part, was much impressed by the work she watched them do.

"What the state of France must have been without the merciful help of the Red Cross," she wrote once, "imagination does not picture. After the armistice was signed, there were removed from Paris, under the auspices of the relief societies, ten thousand wounded men who otherwise must have lingered on in agony, or died from want of care; and there were brought back to French soil nine thousand more who had been cared for in German hospitals."

Later she would tell her friends that she had heard about contributions which generous Americans had sent to Europe, unaware that the bulk of relief supplies there was being dispensed by the Red Cross. Since no arrangements had been made for those American offerings to reach Red Cross authorities, they fell instead into hands not competent to make the best use of them.

"For the most part," Clara Barton reported, "the magnificent charity of America . . . went as unsystematized charity always tends to go, to ruin and to utter waste."

She meant to tell that story when she got home, to prove how necessary it was to organize all charitable ventures. She thought it would be useful in the campaign she was already planning to undertake. She had made up her mind that somehow the United States must be brought into the Red Cross, and made a party to the Geneva Convention.

When Clara Barton finally returned to America, however, she was ill and exhausted again. Some time passed before she was ready to tackle the job she had set herself. A less determined woman would certainly have given it up before it was completed.

She had to overcome Americans' ignorance of the Red Cross itself, and the strong antagonism they felt toward any treaty-like agreement with European powers. She had to find a way to meet objections rooted in the feeling that the United States would never fight another war, and that therefore any preparation for such an event was useless. First of all she had to overcome governmental bureaucracy.

She opened her campaign by presenting to President Rutherford B. Hayes a letter she had asked Moynier to write. It officially invited the United States, once more, to sign and ratify the Convention.

President Hayes was courteous. He assured her that the letter would be referred to the proper authorities in the State Department. Nothing more was ever heard of the communication.

Clara Barton was convinced that the letter had been ignored simply because similar invitations had been turned down in the past, and both times "by *one man*," she complained. Those refusals had established a precedent which she decided could never be broken, so long as that same man remained in his post as an assistant secretary in the State Department.

"There was nothing to hope from that Administration," she decided. Then, early in 1881, James A. Garfield took office as President, and she went to see him immediately. He was a former schoolteacher, like herself. He knew of her work during the Civil War when he had been a major general of the Union forces. His interest in what she had to say was real and personal, and he was completely sympathetic to the humanitarian principles of the Geneva Convention. He did not simply refer her to the State Department. Instead he personally promised that in his first annual message to Congress, at the beginning of the next year, he would urge ratification of the Convention.

The hurdle of bureaucracy was past. It was still necessary to win Congressional and public support.

Clara Barton had already drawn around herself, in Washington, a group of friends and influential supporters. Now they agreed to join with her in a Red Cross Society whose first duty would be to spread information about the Red Cross movement and the international agreement it had brought about. The meeting of that group on May 21, 1881, is now considered the birthday of the American Red Cross. President Garfield publicly approved of the Society, and of the unusual clause Clara Barton wanted to insert into its constitution.

That clause was designed to answer those who said the Red Cross was unnecessary in a nation that never again expected to be involved in any kind of military conflict. It broadened the Society's purpose to include relief to the victims of disasters other than war.

In one of the many addresses she made at the time, Clara Barton admitted it was true that "by our geographical position and isolation, we are far less liable to the disturbances of war than the nations of Europe." But no country, she pointed out, was "more liable than our own to great overwhelming calamaties, various, widespread and terrible . . . Plagues, cholera, fires, flood, famine, all bear upon us with terrible force . . . Like death they are sure to come in some form and at some time, and like it no mortal knows where, how or when."

And America, she declared, had nothing in readiness to meet such emergencies except "the good heart of our people and their impulsive, generous gifts"—gifts that were often less useful than they should be because the country had no "organized system for collection, reception nor distribution."

She reminded her listeners that they supported organized fire departments, to prevent the loss of their homes and factories and schools. Why should they not give equal support to an organization that could prevent the loss of human lives? she asked.

She also told that story about the shiploads of American gifts that had gone largely to waste during the Franco-Prussian War because the senders had not been part of a Red Cross movement. Remaining outside of that movement, and outside of the Geneva Convention, she concluded, was both impractical and unfair to America's standing in the world.

By then four South American countries had joined the Convention, bringing the signers to a total of thirty-one.

"If the United States of America is fortunate and diligent," Clara Barton said, "she may, perhaps, come to stand No. 32

in the roll of civilization and humanity. If not she will remain where she at present stands, among the barbarians and the heathen."

When President Garfield's annual message to Congress was still some months in the future, in August of 1881, he was shot by an assassin. For weeks he lingered between life and death.

Clara Barton was in the little village of Dansville, New York, at the time, at the sanatarium where she often stayed when her health was poor. The villagers told her they knew she had recently been in Washington, doing work that the dying President was interested in. They wanted to know how they could help in that work. Clara Barton organized them on the spot into a local Red Cross Society. Not long afterward, when forest fires spread through Michigan, that little Dansville Society, and the two similar societies just formed in Rochester and Syracuse, New York, stood ready to offer immediate help to the thousands of families left homeless there. Clara Barton directed the program herself.

"Our relief rooms were instantly secured," a Dansville Red Cross member wrote later, "and our white banner, with its bright scarlet cross . . . was thrown to the breeze . . . pointing to every generous heart an outlet for its sympathy. We had not mistaken the spirit of our people; our scarce-opened doorway was filled with men, women and children bearing their gifts of pity and love.

"Tables and shelves were piled," the report went on; "our working committee of ladies took every article under inspection, their faithful hands made all garments whole and strong; lastly, each article received the stamp of the society and of the Red Cross, and all were carefully and quickly consigned to the firm packing cases awaiting them. Eight large boxes were shipped at first, others followed directly, and so continued . . . until no more were needed."

The organization collected and forwarded money too, in

the hands of "a most competent agent, our esteemed towns-man and county clerk."

That same autumn Chester A. Arthur, Garfield's successor, agreed to fulfill the dead President's promise to Clara Barton. Arthur's message to Congress about the Geneva Convention brought about its ratification by Congress the next spring, in March 1882.

A Washington newspaper announced the event in a single four-line paragraph. Except for the handful of people Clara Barton and her friends had been able to reach directly, no American seemed interested in the news. An international agreement for the care of war-wounded had no apparent connection with their own lives. They saw no connection between it and the stories they had recently read about the help sent to fire-devastated Michigan.

The ratification of the Geneva Convention by the United States, a country of rapidly growing power, caused great excitement in Europe, however. Red Cross Societies in many cities lit bonfires in celebration. Moynier sent Clara Barton warm congratulations. And when she arrived in Geneva not long afterward, to attend a conference of Red Cross members, he joined in the tribute that was paid to her.

But he did not approve at all of the American Amendment, as it came to be called—the clause in the American Red Cross constitution which authorized the Society to aid disaster victims. He firmly discouraged other Societies from adopting it.

Henry Dunant himself had suggested years earlier that Red Cross Societies might aid disaster victims during periods between wars. Moynier and the other members of the Geneva Committee had not agreed then. Now Dunant was no longer in a position to put forward his point of view. In 1867 his long-neglected business had gone bankrupt, costing him the respect of various friends whose money had been invested in it. Dunant had immediately resigned from the Committee, to protect it from the glare of the unfavorable publicity suddenly focused on him. Moynier was thus free to carry out his own ideas without strong opposition. Since the Geneva Convention mentioned the Red Cross flag only as a protective symbol for use during war, he said, to use it for any other purpose would be "undoubtedly wrong."

Clara Barton returned to the United States unmoved by his argument. She felt Moynier was being highhanded, and that other Societies could profitably follow the pattern she had already set for America. With remarkable energy for a woman already in her sixties, she set about proving how effective that pattern could be.

She made almost no attempt to enlarge the Red Cross Society she had founded in Washington. She was only slightly interested in encouraging local groups like the one in Dansville. When they did spring up, here and there, she offered them little to do except to raise money and collect food and other supplies when she made public appeals for contributions. As she had once singlehandedly ministered to Civil War wounded, she now personally conducted a relief program every time a disaster occurred that was too big for local charities to handle.

The moment news of one of those disasters reached her, she first made her appeal for contributions through the newspapers. Then she set out herself for the scene of the catastrophe—for the flooded city, the tornado-struck town or the epidemic-ridden area where help was needed. She took with her only a few close friends who soon became her skillful assistants. With their help she estimated the requirements not being met by government agencies, or other bodies, and then swiftly organized her own rather arbitrary system for distributing the supplies she had brought with her.

She could write stirringly of the disasters she witnessed. Newspapers were usually glad to print such accounts as she sent them, and those accounts invariably drew further contributions for the suffering people she regarded as her own responsibility. Her description of an Ohio River flood, for example, told of "surging waters and crashing ice, the floating wrecks of towns and villages, great uprooted giants of the forest plunging madly to the sea, the suddenly unhoused people wandering about the riverbanks, or huddled in strange houses with fireless hearths."

People often resented her. They said she was "bossy." It was certainly true that she liked to run things her own way, and usually did. But sometimes she was criticized unfairly, and by people who had been glad to accept her help. She often had reason to remember what most Red Cross workers have learned at one time or another—that the only way to avoid all criticism is never to dare to act at all. Clara Barton always dared to act.

On the occasion of the tragic Johnstown flood, for example, in the spring of 1889, she was among the first to reach the stricken Pennsylvania city. She found 20,000 people homeless, and sent out a hasty call for lumber with which she had several barracks-like shelters constructed. The buildings were still being used as temporary living quarters when she finally left Johnstown at the end of five exhausting months.

Built with lumber used in barracks after the Johnstown flood, this was the home of the American Red Cross until 1904

Some time later, when the buildings became empty, the owners of the land on which they stood wrote asking Miss Barton to remove them. She sent a representative to Johnstown to superintend the demolition, with instructions to give the lumber to anyone who needed it. Local lumber dealers immediately complained that she was ruining their business. She therefore paid to have the lumber shipped to Washington, to construct a building used first as a warehouse, and later as her home and Red Cross headquarters. And that too brought complaints, this time from people who charged Clara Barton with making private use of money people had contributed to charity.

The American Red Cross National Headquarters today

Time after time, however, in spite of—or perhaps because of—her "bossiness," Clara Barton managed to prove what she most wanted to prove: that the Red Cross offered the most effective channel for the distribution of America's charity. She dispensed that charity to victims of major disasters in every part of the country. She even carried it abroad. When famine struck Russia in 1892, farmers of the Middle West— still grateful for Russia's support of the North during the Civil War—loaded 225 railroad cars with grain and asked Clara Barton to supervise the shipment of their gift. That grain, and other carloads from the same source, went to Russia in the name of the American Red Cross.

As a result of such varied tasks she was prepared for the event that finally brought closer together the two themes of today's universal Red Cross service: wartime aid and aid to sufferers from peacetime disasters.

That event occurred in 1896, when Moslems and Christians were once more fighting in the eastern Mediterranean. Christian Armenians who had revolted against their Turkish rulers were being subjected to severe reprisals. British and American Christian missionaries, appalled at the condition of thousands of starving Armenians, called on their churches to help. Money was raised in large amounts in response to their plea, and food and medicines were purchased. But Turkish authorities refused to allow representatives of Christian institutions to carry those supplies past their lines.

From all over the world waves of sympathy went out to the suffering Armenians, but no way to help them could be devised. Then certain church authorities turned to Clara Barton. As she had once regarded Dr. Appia and his group as uniquely prepared to aid the wounded during the Franco-Prussian War, they now saw her as uniquely fit to help in this crisis. They believed the well-known humanitarian might be admitted to Turkey, a nation which had signed the Geneva

Convention. They knew that, unlike European Red Cross members, she and her assistants possessed ample experience in the complex task of providing food and emergency medical care for thousands of men, women and children.

The success of the American delegation's work among the unfortunate Armenians is now part of Red Cross history. It strengthened the role of the Red Cross as a neutral force able to serve during wartime; it also stressed the value, on the international level, of training and preparation for disaster relief. In spite of Moynier's disapproval, other Red Cross Societies began to take more interest in that kind of service.

Before the nineteenth century came to an end the Red Cross had established itself as a symbol and a reality in most parts of the world. Individual Societies might still be small and weak. But their right to serve on the battlefields of war had been officially recognized by the diplomats who signed the Hague Convention of 1899. This was an international agreement drawn up in the spirit of the Geneva Convention, to lessen the horrors of war by establishing certain rules of warfare to be followed by armies.

Red Cross Societies were also taking the lead in making practical application of the steady advance of modern medicine. They were founding pioneering schools of nursing. They were organizing pioneering first-aid classes to teach volunteers the basic skills of aid to the sick and injured. They were taking turns at calling conferences of Society delegates to discuss and encourage new developments in medical techniques and equipment.

A young Henry Dunant had once felt the need of support for his ideas from the most prominent men and women of Europe. Now those ideas had won world fame for Dunant himself. Penniless after the bankruptcy of his business in 1867, he lived in almost complete obscurity for the next thirty years. Then a journalist, asking questions about a benignly handsome old man in the little Swiss village of

Henry Dunant in 1901

Heiden, learned that the silver-haired patriarch was the author of *A Memory of Solferino*. The journalist's published report of his discovery brought floods of mail and many offers of financial aid to a man whom many had long assumed to be dead.

Dunant never left the peaceful seclusion of Heiden. He died there in 1910, after receiving one of the most distinguished of the many honors eventually bestowed on his name. In 1901 when the first Nobel Peace Prize was awarded, it was divided between two men. One was a Frenchman, Frédéric Passy, founder of a French peace organization. The other was Henry Dunant, the instigator of what many were already describing as the foremost humanitarian achievement of the nineteenth century.

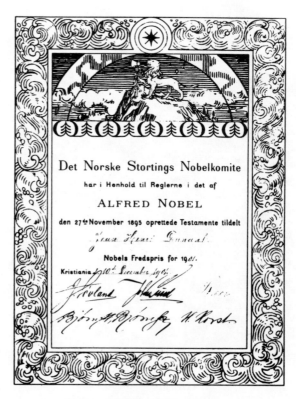

Dunant's Nobel Prize certificate

5. *The Challenge of a World War*

The war that broke out in Europe in August 1914 was the greatest conflict the world had seen until then—and the biggest challenge the Red Cross had faced in its half century of existence. Before that First World War came to an end four years later, all the greatest national powers and many smaller ones were involved in the struggle, and the Red Cross Societies of all those countries had served fighting men and their families in countless ways.

Little boys playing soldier during that war found their small sisters playing Red Cross nurse beside them. With red ribbon crosses on white towels pinned around their heads, and more red crosses on their sleeves, little girls bandaged imaginary wounds under imaginary gunfire. They were acting the role of a heroine the whole world had taken to its heart.

In the many stories written about the Red Cross nurse, she was invariably described as both beautiful and brave. Posters showed her moving like a goddess among the muddy trenches of the battlefields. Soldiers and civilians alike sang a song written to glorify "the rose of no man's land."

In actual fact, at the beginning of the war at least, nurses were not permitted in "no man's land," that shell-ravaged area between the trench lines of the opposing forces. It was the "business of the army," as one British report put it, "to clear up its own battlefields at its own cost and take the wounded to hospital." And the various armies involved in the conflict seemed prepared to carry out that "business" efficiently. The new era of humanity which the Red Cross had helped to bring about, and the rapid advances in medical science, had resulted in vast changes in army medical corps. By 1914 those corps included trained stretcher-bearers, ambulance drivers, doctors and surgeons, all wearing the red cross. Well-supplied hospitals, fleets of ambulances, and mobile first-aid units, also marked with the red cross, had all become part of an army's standard equipment. Navy medical corps were equally well staffed and equipped, and they too had been using the Red Cross symbol since 1906 when a second Geneva Convention applying to naval warfare had been signed by most major world powers.

Many military authorities believed, therefore, that the Red Cross had outlived its usefulness as a "relief society" for active service under fire. The only tasks left to the Red Cross, as these authorities saw it, were to staff hospitals behind the lines, and to give patients in those hospitals whatever extra comforts could be purchased out of public contributions.

If the war that started in 1914 had followed the pattern of the previous "little wars" in Europe, the role of the Red Cross might have been limited to those two tasks alone.

But this was not a "little war." As the fighting continued, month after month, the forces on both sides swelled to hundreds of thousands and then to millions. They fought on a western front that stretched far across France, on an eastern front that cut through Poland and into Russia. They fought in Italy and Africa and in the eastern Mediterranean. Japanese and German battalions fought in China over German interests there.

Casualties mounted **higher each** day—and medical corps-

A World War I Red Cross poster

men were often among them. Their red cross arm bands had not protected them from shells fired at long range by enemies far beyond sight of their targets.

More nurses were needed near the fronts, and the Red Cross was called on. Soon it was being called on for many other reasons too.

Military authorities came to realize that a war-weary soldier needed help of a kind the army was not prepared to give. He needed writing materials and books, candy and cigarettes, an occasional hour of recreation, a nonmilitary friend willing to listen to his troubles. The Red Cross could supply those things, and it did.

And when whole villages were shelled to the ground, leaving homeless refugees for whom armies felt responsible but whom they could not help, the Red Cross fed and housed and clothed those people too.

In the meantime, behind the front lines, Red Cross volunteers were taking on countless new duties on their own. They set up recreation centers where soldiers far from home could meet old friends and make new ones. They offered convalescent care to men recently released from hospitals. They helped soldiers keep in touch with their families, and gave aid of many kinds to the families whose breadwinner was fighting or wounded, or who had been killed or taken prisoner. They knitted sweaters and scarves, folded bandages and made many other articles which hard-pressed manufacturers could not turn out fast enough to meet the military's more and more urgent demands.

The various National Red Cross Societies brought different degrees of wealth and skill to their jobs, depending on their size and pre-war experience.

The German Red Cross, for example, was both large and widely experienced. The organizations which had united to form it, when Prussia and various smaller states united in the German Empire after the Franco-Prussian War, included some of the oldest and most active "relief societies" of Europe.

The Japanese Society had existed since 1877, and it too was large, with a membership of over 2 million before the war. It had earned a reputation for maintaining excellent standards of nursing.

French and Italian Societies had their own hospitals, established in most cases by wealthy and titled women who headed the Red Cross in those countries. The hospital sponsors, untrained themselves in medicine and administration, had often been content to hire women untrained in hygiene or care of the sick. But during World War II many of those hospitals improved even as they grew overcrowded, because directors and staffs came under the influence of other Red Cross people with higher professional standards.

The British Red Cross Society had been recognized, before the war, as the official channel through which England's War Office would accept volunteer aid. The War Office, however, reluctant to attach volunteers to its own excellent medical services, had suggested that the Red Cross confine itself to providing V.A.D's—Voluntary Aid Detachments—to the home-defense organization. The suggestion was not flattering. No one took the home-defense organization very seriously in the pre-war years; no one expected it to be called to active duty in the foreseeable future. Nevertheless the Red Cross had agreed. So did the St. John's Society, the volunteer group which had pioneered in introducing civilian first aid work in Britain, similar to some done in the United States by the American Red Cross. Before the war began the two organizations together had trained more than 2,000 V.A.D.'s in first aid, sanitation, nursing, ambulance driving, cooking and other work. That training made those units enormously valuable when the War Office was forced to enlist their help soon after hostilities began. Transporting the wounded was only one of the responsibilities the V.A.D.'s took over and carried out superbly.

Like most Red Cross Societies, the British group grew rapidly during the war and raised enormous amounts of money. It built up a war library of some 6 million books which it distributed among the sick and wounded. It sent launches to Mesopotamia to carry home casualties from the battlefields there. Along with the Societies of Canada, India and other members of what is now the British Commonwealth, it gave large grants to hospitals, bought and equipped ambulances, and opened up small auxiliary nursing centers for convalescents in thousands of private homes.

Until 1917 the United States remained a neutral, not

actively involved in the war. But the American Red Cross, like the national Red Cross Society of neutral Switzerland, offered its help to all belligerent nations under the terms of the Geneva Conventions as soon as the war started.

Two facts seemed to suggest that the help the Americans could supply would be limited.

First, their Society was very small compared to most European organizations. Efforts had been made to start new chapters in various parts of the country, after Clara Barton's "one-woman" society came to an end with her retirement in 1904. But the national leaders who took her place—including the President of the United States, now officially head of the Red Cross—were a handful of socially prominent and wealthy men and women. They saw little need for a large organization of ordinary citizens. The new chapters that had been formed usually consisted of only a few leaders in each community, people willing to aid in disaster-fund drives in return for the prestige that Red Cross work gave them. In 1914 less than 17,000 Americans had contributed the annual dollar or more which made them members of the National Society.

Second, the Society's only previous war experience had been during the brief Spanish-American War of 1898. Since then it had been officially chartered as the one volunteer agency on which the Army could call in time of need, but the Army had never required its services. Most Americans therefore—and the rest of the world as well—still thought of the Society's sole function as disaster relief.

Two other facts, however, made the role of the American Red Cross during the First World War vastly important.

One was the American public's willingness to contribute generously to any appeal for help.

The other was the remarkable progress made by the Society's new leadership toward raising the standards of nursing. Professional schools of nursing were just then coming into their own. Many women who wanted to become nurses were still enrolling in inferior schools, or hiring themselves out to hospitals without any training at all. But the leaders of the Red Cross used the weight of their authority to improve the poorer schools, encourage the best ones, and discourage the use of untrained women in hospitals. The nurses on the roster they maintained, ready to serve in any emergency, were all graduates of accredited schools—a nursing elite whose influence was already spreading throughout the country. By 1914 that roster contained 5,500 names.

So it was possible for the American Red Cross to respond with surprising speed when most of the belligerent nations accepted its offer of help.

Ten medical units, each one consisting of a dozen nurses and three surgeons, were assembled almost immediately. Funds raised, after an appeal by the President, provided equipment and chartered a ship that was hastily painted with huge red cross emblems. The "Mercy Ship," as she came to be called, carried those highly trained Red Cross teams to Europe within six weeks after war had been declared.

For more than a year those units, and others that followed them abroad, served in hospitals for the wounded in England, Belgium, France, Germany, Austria, Serbia and Russia. In many places they introduced for the first time really modern standards of hygiene and medical care. The American nurses never hesitated to get down on their knees to scrub floors, or work up to their elbows in disinfecting suds, if the building that had been assigned to them as a hospital needed a thorough cleaning. One unit working in Russia was delighted when several Russian aristocrats decided to clean their own hospital in what they described as "the American way," and to bathe their patients as carefully as they had seen the American nurses do.

Then, on February 3, 1917, the United States broke diplomatic relations with Germany, and openly declared her sympathy with Germany's foes. Patriotism swept through the country like a raging fire. Men rushed to enlist in an Expeditionary Force. The official declaration of war occurred on April 6th. A well-known banker, Henry P. Davison, agreed to head a Red Cross War Council. By then the American Red Cross was already being transformed from a weakling child into a giant.

A single Connecticut town, within two weeks, took in 18,000 new members—more than there had been in the entire country a few years earlier.

A drive to raise the then-staggering sum of 100 million dollars was not only reached but topped within a matter of weeks.

Long before the first American soldier set foot on a European battlefield, the American Red Cross was at the front, still ready to aid the wounded of both sides, but working now strictly within the lines of America's allies. In France, for example, it eventually set up more than fifty field hospitals for which it purchased the equipment and recruited the personnel—hospitals that formed a substantial contribution to a rapidly expanding Army Medical Corps.

The first and one of the largest programs it undertook was to aid the French Red Cross, an organization utterly exhausted after three terrible years of war. Americans helped operate its canteens, and soon opened their own canteens for French soldiers. American nurses and field workers spent American dollars to aid thousands of penniless refugees from the German-occupied parts of the country, refugees whom the French Red Cross could no longer afford to support.

American volunteers drove American ambulances over the mountainous roads of northern Italy, helping to transport the casualties that numbered over 300,000 after the disastrous battle of Caporetto. Several of those drivers were wounded. All were later decorated by the Italian government for heroism. One of the most severaly wounded was a nine-

An American Red Cross canteen at Bordeaux

teen-year-old boy from Illinois, Ernest Hemingway, whose *Farewell to Arms,* published ten years later, gave the world a novelist's vivid impressions of the Red Cross in action.

Henry Dunant's dream of world peace, born after another Italian hill battle over half a century earlier, seemed farther from reality than ever. But the First World War was transforming his "relief societies" into organizations far larger and more effective than he could ever have dreamed.

When the first American soldiers set sail for Europe, they were already accustomed to depending on the Red Cross for help. While they had been learning to obey new commands, and handle strange weapons, thousands of Red Cross volunteers had been learning how to serve them.

Homesick soldiers staring out of the windows of a train had prompted Red Cross volunteers to offer them coffee and doughnuts served from a station platform. Soon military authorities took it for granted that traveling soldiers would always be fed by the Red Cross units set up in 700 locations throughout the country. America's Red Cross canteen service followed the men abroad too, where it served them a total of some 6 million meals, and provided them with countless other services in the 130 canteens it established for Americans in France alone.

A doughboy, bound for a port of embarkation, is served by a canteen worker

During their first days in camp the worried soldiers who needed emergency passes, or faced unexpected crises in their personal lives, had learned that their unit had its own Red Cross Field Director, a man whose only job was to help them solve their problems. That Field Director also went abroad when the unit moved, to risk the same dangers and discomforts the soldiers endured—although he had almost invariably been classified as too old or physically unfit for military service.

Sick and wounded soldiers, of course, came to know at firsthand the skills of the professional Red Cross nurse and doctor, and the tireless willingness of all the other Red Cross volunteers who worked beside them in the medical services.

A Red Cross worker comforts a wounded soldier awaiting transportation to a field hospital

Even soldiers who were captured knew that they had not been forgotten by the Red Cross. Volunteers from their own national Society could not follow them through the gates of an enemy prison camp, but inside those gates there was still the chance that they could keep in touch with their families through the International Committee of the Red Cross—the ICRC.

That Swiss Committee no longer had to send delegates like Dr. Appia to the front to aid the wounded. Now, with wounded men and those who cared for them all protected as "neutrals" under the Geneva Conventions, the ICRC was free to pioneer in a new direction on behalf of prisoners of war.

At that time prisoners were afforded only the meager protection provided by a Hague Convention signed by most world powers in 1907. That agreement did set up standards for the humane treatment of captives. It also required a nation at war to establish an information bureau capable of answering queries about the prisoners it held. But mail could not cross enemy lines, once a war had started. A French family could not write to the German bureau to obtain news of a captured son; a German family could not obtain information directly through a bureau in Paris. So the ICRC, taking the initiative again as it had done in the past, established its own Information Agency to serve as a clearinghouse for such queries.

A French family wanting news of its son could therefore write to the ICRC and its Agency would try to obtain the desired information. If the German bureau could not supply it, or failed to forward it, the ICRC's staff of volunteers made every effort to obtain it on their own. Sometimes they wrote dozens of letters, each addressed to a soldier known to be in the "lost" man's regiment, in the hope of learning what had happened to him.

It was tedious work, but most of the people who volun-

Supplies are distributed to the people of Islay, Scotland, who took the survivors of the troopship Otranto *into their homes*

An outpost station in the Argonne Forest, October, 1918

teered for it remained on duty week in and week out for the duration of the war. The majority of them were Swiss. The rest were foreigners who happened to be in Switzerland at the time—such men as the brilliant French novelist Romain Rolland, whose hatred of war made him willing to labor at any task designed to relieve suffering, rather than to support the war effort of his own government.

The Information Agency in Geneva also helped transmit messages directly from a captive's family to the captive himself, and provided delivery service for the relief parcels which—according to the Hague Convention—prisoners were entitled to receive. Thousands of pounds of food, clothing, books and other articles contributed by National Red Cross Societies thus found their way into the hands of men in prison camps.

The ICRC Information Agency in Geneva in 1914

A volunteer worker checks prisoner of war lists

The Swiss delegates who delivered those parcels often had the opportunity to see how the prisoners were being treated, and to make suggestions for improving conditions in camps where the food or shelter did not seem in keeping with the provisions of the Hague Convention. Sometimes their suggestions were accepted, out of respect for the principles the delegates represented; sometimes they were not.

But usually these inspections had at least some beneficial results, and delegates made them whenever they were permitted to do so. That was one of the reasons why the ICRC was awarded, in 1917, the same Nobel Peace Prize that Henry Dunant had been given sixteen years earlier.

Dunant had believed, in the years just before his death, that the Geneva Convention had united nations in a common purpose to "study the means of putting a curb on the brutalities of war, and to create instead a striving to vie with each other—nations, peoples, and races, in dedication to humanity." The First World War had proved how far nations still were from vying with each other in dedication to humanity; it had also proved that even in the midst of war's brutalities, the Red Cross could keep alive the principles on which Dunant had built his belief.

6. New Programs for the Red Cross

The signing of an armistice on November 11, 1918, bringing the First World War officially to an end, did not mean the end of the ICRC's work. For many more months it was occupied with the massive task of helping to repatriate thousands of war prisoners, and extending what aid it could to refugees straggling back to homes they had fled days or years before.

As always in the past, the ICRC had been able to enlist the services of Swiss lawyers, bankers, men in almost every profession and business, who were willing to put aside their own affairs to undertake missions for the Red Cross. But the ICRC had not always been able to win that same kind of willing co-operation from the governments of the warring nations. One obstacle was the limited scope of international agreements like the Geneva and the Hague Conventions. None of these agreements, for example, officially authorized prison-camp inspection by neutral delegates. And no agreement offered any protection at all to civilians during wartime.

Even before the war ended, therefore, the legal experts who worked for or with the ICRC had been preparing new draft agreements for the consideration of the world's governments.

Max Huber, President of the International Committee of the Red Cross, 1928–1946

One of those agreements, eventually signed by most world powers in 1929, spelled out more clearly the rights of prisoners of war. To guarantee that those rights be granted, the representatives of their protecting powers were authorized to visit prisoners in the camps where they were held. (A protecting power is the nation which takes over responsibility for another nation's affairs during a war or a period of broken diplomatic relations. When relations were broken between the United States and Cuba in 1961, for example, the United States asked Switzerland to look after its interests in Cuba. Switzerland thus became the protecting power for American citizens on Cuban soil.)

The agreement also called for the establishment, during wartime, of a prisoner information bureau in some neutral country. It expressly stated that the ICRC might offer to set up such a bureau itself, whenever it deemed this necessary.

The 1929 agreement added, however, that by assigning the

ICRC that one wartime task, it did not mean to set up any obstacles to other humanitarian work the ICRC might perform "for the protecting of prisoners of war with the consent of the belligerents concerned." This gave the Committee the right to propose other tasks it might wish to undertake. It might offer to co-operate with various protecting powers in their camp-visit programs, or to do other things necessary for prisoners' welfare.

The ICRC also drew up another draft agreement with the purpose of extending some protection to civilian noncombatants in wartime. The agreement was eventually presented to the world powers at an international conference in Tokyo in 1934, but it was not signed at the time.

World War I, in other words, had proved to the ICRC that more remained to be done in the future to carry forward the work its predecessors had begun in 1863. And because the Committee still regarded itself as the guardian of the principles of the Red Cross, it continued its job of trying to extend those principles into new areas.

The Armistice of 1918 did not put an end to the work of the Red Cross Societies either. They too were involved in aid to refugees and in helping to repatriate prisoners. Their hospitals and medical staffs were overburdened at the time, not only with wounded men, but also with the victims of a severe influenza epidemic. Both the sick and the wounded had to be cared for until they could be transported home, and there too thousands would continue to need care for many months, perhaps for many years. Even healthy soldiers still looked to their Field Directors and to Red Cross canteens during their journey home and, in the weeks before their demobilization, for the day-to-day comforts on which they had come to depend.

Not all soldiers praised the Red Cross unreservedly at the war's end. Some Americans complained, for example, that they had been asked to pay for food they ate at Red Cross

A transit camp in Narwa, Estonia, for the repatriation of prisoners of war

canteens, though their families at home had been contributing money to the Red Cross in the belief that they were providing free food at those centers. It was true that some American Red Cross canteens did ask payment for the meals they served, but this was because the military authorities had told them to do so. And the authorities had made their demand with reason, usually in connection with a canteen set up near privately owned restaurants.

If the owner of a French restaurant had complained that a free canteen was ruining his business, Red Cross workers might be told to charge for the meals they served in order to preserve friendly relations with French civilians. But the prices charged were always small, and no penniless soldier was ever turned away hungry—though penniless American doughboys were rare because their rate of pay was far higher than that of soldiers of other nationalities.

Soldiers also sometimes claimed that they knew men who had paid for sweaters made of Red Cross yarn, knitted by Red Cross volunteers, and intended as free gifts to men in uniform. The truth in such cases was that the Red Cross did, in fact, give away all the sweaters and other garments which came into its hands. But a soldier who wanted an extra dollar or two, to spend during a leave, might sell his sweater to another man—and thus the story would be born that a man had "paid" for his Red Cross sweater.

Still, in spite of their complaints, most soldiers admitted that the Red Cross, compared to any other volunteer organization working among the armed forces, gave "the best to the most" as someone put it.

The signing of the Armistice, which had so little effect on the work load of the ICRC and of the National Societies, did serve as a signal that set in motion a brand-new Red Cross program. The program was proposed by Henry Davison, director of the American Red Cross War Council.

Davison had watched the American Society grow, in four years, from less than 17,000 members, most of them prominent social leaders in their communities, to more than 20 million people in every walk of life. He knew Red Cross groups in other lands had also grown during the War. Perhaps most importantly, he had witnessed the dramatic development of a Junior Red Cross.

Children had long been sympathetically stirred by the movement. Ontario youngsters had formed a club to help Canadian Red Cross efforts on behalf of victims of the 1899–1902 Boer War. Even earlier, during the Ohio River flood of 1884, American boys and girls had given money to Clara Barton for the homeless victims of that disaster. One group of six boys and girls of Waterford, Pennsylvania, became famous for their generous gesture. They organized an entertainment, raised $51.25, and sent it to Clara Barton with the request that it be used to help people who especially needed

Henry P. Davison

aid. Miss Barton had chosen the recipients of that particular gift very carefully; they were a widow and her own six children, living in a corncrib in a sea of mud because their own home had been washed away. And at Clara Barton's suggestion the river landing at that point, where the children's money helped to raise a new home, was marked with a hand-lettered sign reading LITTLE SIX RED CROSS LANDING.

Many newspapers related the story of that gift and its results. Some printed the letter sent afterward to Clara Barton by the fund raisers. It said:

"We thank you for going to so much trouble in putting our money just where we would have put it ourselves.

"Sometime again when you want money to help you in your good work, call on the 'Little Six'.

But the first real founders of what had become an organized Junior Red Cross were two groups of young people who had decided to help the Red Cross during the first days of the First World War. One group was in New South Wales, Australia. The other was in Saskatchewan, Canada. Neither was aware of what the other was doing. Each began its work spontaneously.

By 1919, in those two countries, and in the United States as well, the Junior Red Cross was taking real shape. The next year its first two magazines appeared, one Canadian, one American. By then the movement already had 8 million members in the United States, and Junior units were beginning to spring up in many other lands.

Davison was a man accustomed to success. At nineteen he had started work as a runner for a bank in Bridgeport, Connecticut. At thirty-two he was president of a bank in New York—the youngest bank president in the country. By the time the war had begun he was well known in circles of international finance. When he put aside his own affairs to devote himself to the Red Cross, it was perhaps not surprising that the Society's fund drives were enormously successful.

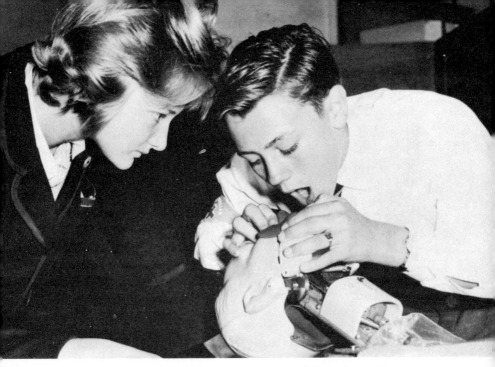

Two Australian Juniors practice the "mouth-to-mouth" method of artificial respiration

Thailand Juniors learn infant care

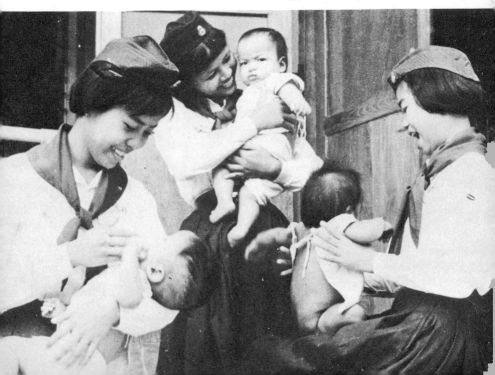

But in Davison's eyes the Red Cross was important chiefly in its role of an immense "army of mercy," as one of his business friends called it. And it seemed to him that this recently expanded army, cutting across national boundary lines and lines of race and color, should not be demobilized at the end of the war that had brought it into being—even if that conflict did prove to be, as people everywhere were hoping in 1919, the final war to end war.

Battle wounds had never been the only cause of suffering in the world. Mankind had already discovered, in fact, that they were less dangerous killers than disease: the 1918 influenza epidemic alone had caused more deaths than all the recently silenced guns of the opposing armies.

Similar epidemics might break out anywhere, at any time. Famine was a constant menace to mankind. Natural disasters, such as floods and hurricanes, brought suffering to some corner of the world almost every day in the year.

Red Cross Juniors from different countries helped build the Henry Dunant House in the Netherlands, a meeting place for all Juniors

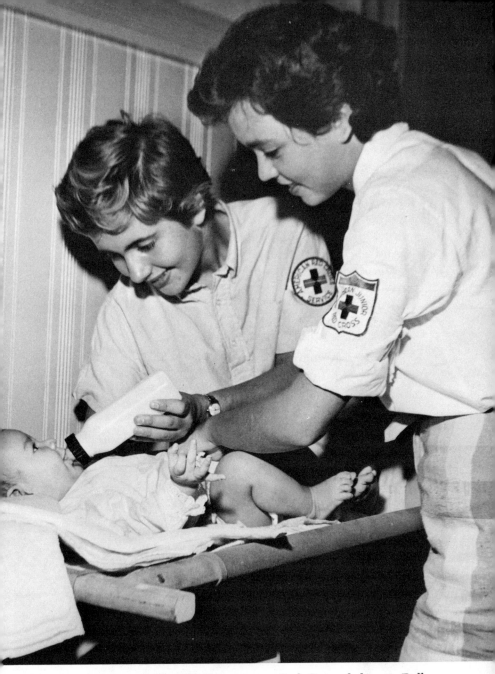

Two Juniors provide nursery care at a Red Cross shelter in Dallas, Texas, after 1961 Hurricane Carla

For those reasons, therefore, Davison suggested that the Red Cross Societies of the world join forces for an international campaign that would be the first of its kind. It would attack suffering, on a scale Clara Barton had scarcely imagined, wherever suffering existed. Its goal would be no less than "the general welfare of humanity."

"While the Governments are arranging a political peace," Davison said, "let the Red Cross Societies of the world come together in a union and add the weight of the Red Cross spirit to the reconciliation which should succeed this war."

And so, while diplomats were designing the League of Nations in the hope of outlawing war, a new League of Red Cross Societies came into being in 1919. Davison was the first chairman of its board. Its headquarters were established in Geneva, which by then had come to be recognized as a sort of humanitarian capital of the world.

With the formation of that League the pattern of today's International Red Cross was essentially complete. It con-

Juniors review their roles in a disaster operation to prepare themselves for future emergencies

sisted then, as it does now, of four separate and distinct parts: the International Committee of the Red Cross, the individual national Red Cross Societies, the new League, and a Conference bringing together both government and Red Cross representatives.

A word about each of those four parts may help to clarify a pattern which is both vast and complex.

The ICRC—the International Committee of the Red Cross —is the oldest part of the pattern. It no longer has only five members as it had in the beginning. Today it consists of anywhere from twenty to twenty-five persons, not counting its small paid staff and the dozens, sometimes thousands, of workers—volunteer and paid—it can call on at a moment's notice. All the Committeemen are still Swiss: when one of them dies or retires, the others name another Swiss citizen to fill his unpaid post. Past and present Committee members include some of the most distinguished citizens of the country— statesmen, doctors, lawyers and educators.

The word *International* in the Committee's name thus has nothing to do with its members: it is not the Committee's personnel that is international, but its program. Because it is the only group of private citizens in the world whose neutrality has never been questioned, it has been able to carry Red Cross principles into every part of the globe.

Its regular paid staff, just large enough to handle its legal and administrative work, is not accustomed to lavish accommodations. At the time of the ICRC's centenary year it occupied a former hotel, a handsome structure with a magnificent view of Lake Geneva and a spacious reception room that invariably impressed visitors—but with few of the conveniences of a modern office building. Renovation, like the purchase of a new headquarters, was regarded as beyond the Committee's budget, which is met chiefly by the contributions of National Societies and a few national governments.

ORGANIZATION OF THE RED CROSS

States party
to the
Geneva Conventions

The International Committee of the Red Cross (Founder body, neutral intermediary in cases of conflict)	International Conference of the Red Cross (Red Cross Parliament)	The League of Red Cross Societies (Federation of National Societies)
	National Red Cross (Red Crescent, Red Lion and Sun) Societies	

Diagram taken from *The International Red Cross*, by Henri Coursier, published by the International Committee of the Red Cross, Geneva, 1961

Staff members do not expect to travel luxuriously either. One lawyer, dispatched on an emergency mission, was so astonished to find himself in a first-class plane seat that he thought a mistake had been made. Then he realized that all the second-class seats must have been booked at the time his own last-minute reservation was made. Afterward he claimed that the unusual comfort of that journey made the mission memorable to him, though to others it was memorable for a different reason: he had been requested to travel halfway around the world to accept the release of some 250 prisoners being held by the revolutionary forces fighting a certain dictatorship. The dictator himself had at first flatly refused to admit the prisoners' existence, because he was still publicly insisting that no armed force opposed his rule; a week of patient discussion was thus needed before the dictator's cooperation could be assured, after which the delegate still had to travel many miles across flooded rivers and through ambush-infested hills to the designated exchange site. When he reached it he walked forward, alone and unarmed, to meet the prisoners and their guards. Then, at last, he successfully piloted the men over those same long difficult miles to the nation's capital where they were reunited with their families. His mission completed, he took off once more for Geneva— traveling that time, as usual, in a second-class seat.

Next oldest of the four parts of the International Red Cross are the individual Societies. Their number has changed over the years as newly independent nations establish their own Societies, or when two or more nations unite into one and their originally separate Societies combine into a single organization.

Not all are known as Red Cross Societies. Moslem Turkey, for example, unwilling to use the symbol of a cross even though the Red Cross was never intended to have any specifically Christian significance, chose as its own symbol the red crescent of its flag, and calls its organization the Red

Members of Turkey's National Red Crescent Society conduct a clinic in a rural area

Crescent Society. Other Moslem countries (Afghanistan, Iraq, Jordan, Libya, Morocco, Sudan, Tunisia and the United Arab Republic) decided to use the same name. But these Societies, like the one in Turkey, remain in the framework of the International Red Cross.

Iran, another Moslem nation, also took its own name and symbol from its flag, and thus brought a third name into the roster of National Societies. Its Red Lion and Sun Society became particularly familiar to the rest of the world in September, 1962, when it supervised the distribution of the relief supplies that poured into Iran that year for the benefit of earthquake victims. A particularly severe quake had devastated a wide area, killing 11,000 Iranians, destroying or damaging more than 100 villages and leaving 30,000 people homeless.

The Personnel Committee of the League of Red Cross Societies in 1919

No further names, however, are likely to be added to the Red Cross family, because the Societies have agreed that new units in the future will not be authorized to use any name other than Red Cross.

Some National Societies receive government support. Others—like the American Red Cross—do not, although their charters may require them to undertake certain tasks at governmental request.

The third part of the international whole, the League of Red Cross Societies, is supported by contributions from the various member societies. Its board of governors, consisting of a representative from each Society, lays down the League's general program which is carried out by a staff of paid employees drawn from many nations.

That program is divided into sections, each with its own bureau in the Geneva headquarters: Nursing, Relief, and Medico-Social. The Bureaus help Societies develop their own programs, supply them with materials and expert advice, and serve as clearinghouses for the exchange of information. There is a Bureau of the Junior Red Cross too, which helps to organize and develop programs for young people. And there is an Information and Publications Bureau which is always especially busy just before World Red Cross Day on the eighth day of May each year.

The fourth part of the International Red Cross is the Conference, usually held every four years, when delegates from the ICRC, the various Societies and the League all meet with representatives of the governments which are parties to the Geneva Conventions. This Conference reaches decisions on all questions of common interest, recommends general lines of activity for the Red Cross as a whole, and ensures the unity of its efforts.

Henry Dunant once said that his ideas could be expressed in three simple words: *people helping people*. That phrase exactly describes the work of the Red Cross since the formation of the League. Then it became for the first time a truly world-wide organization of people willing to contribute their time and their talents to help other people in need—who, in their turn, stand ready to offer help when they are able.

After a hurricane strikes the Gulf Coast of the United States, for example, many of its victims may receive Red Cross help. And within a year those same people may be giving help to the victims of a landslide in Peru or a flood in the Netherlands.

Co-operation is not always easy to learn, and many Societies had no experience in disaster relief. Nevertheless the members of the new League began to work together almost immediately in many different fields. They took part in the typhus-control campaign in Europe in 1919; they helped

Civil Defense and Red Cross workers join the National Guard in rescuing Gulf Coast residents during Hurricane Carla

feed hungry people in revolution-torn Russia during a famine in 1921; they aided the homeless and the injured after earthquakes struck Chile, Colombia, Costa Rica, Japan and Persia, all in the single year of 1923.

Some member Societies of the League worked for a time through an international disaster relief union sponsored by the League of Nations. But the ties that bound together the League of Red Cross Societies proved more durable than those binding the governments of nations in their League. When, in 1939, the world exploded into another and even more frightful World War, the League of Nations was shattered, but the League of Red Cross Societies maintained its disaster-relief program even during that conflict, at a time when it was working together with the ICRC in massive war projects.

It is true that in the Second World War military medical services were in actual fact as well equipped as they had wrongly assumed themselves to be at the start of the First World War; they did not therefore require the aid of the Red Cross to set up hospitals and first-aid stations at the front. But they did require the aid of Red Cross Societies in preparing millions of surgical dressings and in collecting the millions of pints of blood that saved countless lives.

And during that war the Red Cross was asked to provide, on an immense scale, the same kind of canteen and morale-building services it had given earlier. It was called upon to furnish aid to the war prisoners, who enormously outnumbered those of the First World War. Its assistance to civilian war victims was on such a huge scale that it could never be measured in human terms.

Yet during the war years 1939–1945 the National Red Cross Societies also responded to appeals for help from nearly a dozen countries which, in that same period, suffered from cyclones and hurricanes, earthquakes and floods.

The pattern for reaction to such disasters had already been set. It functioned during the war as it had functioned earlier. Usually, when catastrophe struck, the National Red Cross Society of the afflicted country sent a request for help to Geneva. Or the Geneva officials of the ICRC and the League might telephone or cable a query as to whether outside assistance was required. In either case, once the need for aid was known, joint telegrams from the two Geneva offices went out to those member Societies considered best able to respond to a particular appeal.

An earthquake struck Greece in 1941, for example, and immediately the Greek Red Cross Society received a telegram from Geneva asking if help was needed. The answer was yes. The Geneva offices then jointly sent twelve National Societies invitations to aid Greece. Not one failed to respond. All gave generously.

The Latin motto of the Red Cross, *Inter arma caritas*, is usually translated as "In the midst of battle, charity." The Second World War established the fact that this organization, founded to alleviate suffering on the battlefield, had finally and fully committed itself to a far wider program. In the midst of battles more destructive than any men had known before, the Red Cross did not forget that it had grown into a movement pledged to the alleviation of all suffering, everywhere.

7. The Red Cross in World War II

On September 1, 1939, the German Nazi army of Adolf Hitler invaded Poland. England and France immediately declared themselves at war with Germany, as Poland's allies. World War II had begun. Before it ended, almost six years later, it would involve more than fifty nations, more than 65 million fighting men, and tens of millions of civilians.

The communication which the ICRC quickly sent out to each newly belligerent nation had certain specific purposes.

First, the ICRC was offering its own services on behalf of the war's victims, as it was privileged to do under the Geneva Conventions in their 1929 form. The Committee was ready to open an agency for the exchange of information about prisoners of war; it had, in fact, already acquired space and a volunteer staff for such an agency. It was equally ready to send its delegates to inspect prison camps and hospitals. It was prepared to organize a mail service that would function across battle lines, and a system for distributing drugs, food and other supplies to prisoners.

But the Committee could not perform any of those services without the co-operation of the belligerents. It was therefore seeking that co-operation at the first posssible moment.

The ICRC was also asking the belligerents to agree to live up to the provisions of the 1934 Tokyo Draft, even though that suggested extension of the Geneva Conventions had never been ratified. The Tokyo Draft had been drawn up to provide "captured" civilians with at least as much protection as was granted to captured soldiers. It applied both to the citizens of a conquered nation and to people living in a foreign country at the time that country went to war against their own homeland. The Japanese living in the United States at the time America declared war on Japan, for example, belonged to this second group usually spoken of as "enemy aliens."

The governments which had already signed the 1929 Geneva Conventions—they included all the eventual belligerents of World War II except Soviet Russia, Finland and Japan—replied promptly to the ICRC's communications. They pledged to live up to those 1929 agreements, and declared themselves willing to listen to any specific suggestions the ICRC might make about carrying out its humanitarian program. They were willing to co-operate with a prisoner of war agency in neutral Switzerland. They did not, any of them, agree to abide by the Tokyo Draft.

The ICRC, still determined to obtain some protection for civilian victims of the war, promptly sent out further communications. This time it was trying specifically to win protection for at least those comparatively small groups of people each belligerent was holding as enemy aliens. There were German enemy aliens being held in England, for example; there were English enemy aliens being held in Germany. The ICRC suggested that all the governments agree, on a reciprocal or even-Stephen basis, to give those interned civilians the same protection granted ordinary prisoners of war.

Often in the past the ICRC had successfully obtained this sort of reciprocal agreement by pointing out that each side gained—that neither lost—by such an arrangement. It succeeded this time too. Almost all the belligerents finally agreed to treat civilian internees humanely, to permit them to receive mail and relief packages, and to have contact with delegates of their protecting power and of the ICRC. This agreement ultimately affected some 150,000 persons.

But the ICRC could not persuade the belligerents to extend equal rights to the masses of people living in enemy-occupied countries. When Germany invaded and conquered part of Poland, for example, she claimed that the inhabitants of that region had become German subjects whose fate was strictly an "internal affair" of the German government. Thus Germany did as she wished with the Poles—herded them into concentration camps, used them as slave labor, starved them, murdered them—and flatly refused the ICRC any right to interfere on their behalf.

There were many things the ICRC failed to do during the war. There were prison camps its delegates were unable to enter. There were violations of the Geneva Conventions it was powerless to prevent. There were millions of civilians, in desperate need, to whom it could distribute none of the food, clothing and medical supplies piled up in Red Cross warehouses.

The Committee's failures are scarcely surprising in view of the fact that this tiny group of civilians, poor in funds and facilities, had no force except a moral one, no weapons except persistence and persuasion. What is surprising is that the Committee accomplished as much as it did.

Some of its achievments can be reduced to bald statistics.

During the six years of the war it distributed, to captured soldiers and to civilian internees, more than 450,000 tons of relief supplies worth over 750 million dollars.

These supplies included millions of individual relief parcels; the American Red Cross alone packed over 27 million such parcels for the ICRC to forward. Some parcels were addressed to specific individuals, in care of the ICRC in Geneva,

The S.S. Caritas *is loaded with Red Cross relief supplies at Philadelphia*

Prisoner relief boxes in a Geneva warehouse

and had to be re-addressed and sent on their way. Others were in bulk lots whose shipment presented staggering problems at a time when the seas were infested with submarines, rail lines were regularly bombed, and freight cars and trucks became scarcer every week.

The sum of 3½ million dollars needed to pay the transportation and warehouse costs of that program, like the cost of the supplies themselves, was contributed by National Red Cross Societies, by belligerent governments intent on caring for their own captured soldiers, and by neutral countries eager to ease the sufferings of all war victims.

The ICRC, whose annual pre-war income was a meager $30,000, spent a further 13 million dollars on its prison-information service, its camp-visiting program, and other humane activities. Half that amount came from world-wide sources, including those belligerents who had most to gain from the Committee's efforts. The other half was donated by the

An ICRC delegate distributes relief parcels to French prisoners of war in Germany

people and the government of neutral Switzerland. With that money, equal to the cost of running the war itself for just six hours, the ICRC kept thousands of people physically alive, and prevented millions more from retreating into the emotional death of despair or insanity.

In response to desperate appeals from Greece the ICRC also directed the feeding of almost the entire population of that tragically ravaged country all during World War II. This unique civilian relief program—unique, that is, for the ICRC in wartime—was organized only after elaborate negotiations with Greece's conqueror, Germany, and with the Allied nations that were blockading her ports. Further equally elaborate negotiations were necessary before arrangements could be completed for importing the needed supplies by Swedish and Turkish freighters, by small Greek sailing ships, and by various other emergency means.

Five thousand persons were eventually at work manning that Greek relief program. They distributed 700,000 tons of food, 500 tons of medicines and medical equipment, and more than 200,000 gallons of diet-enriching cod-liver oil.

Of all the projects the ICRC undertook during the war, none better illustrates its flexibility and inventiveness than the Central Agency for Prisoners of War.

The official purpose of this Agency can be described in a single sentence: It was to serve as a kind of general post office for receiving and distributing official information about prisoners. Its work seemed simple enough.

The Agency was supposed to receive lists of prisoners' names automatically. They were to come from the information bureau which the Geneva Conventions required each belligerent nation to establish. Then the Agency was supposed to forward those lists to the government of each country whose soldiers or civilians had been captured.

In a hall of the Palace of the General Council in Geneva, the Central Agency for Prisoners begins its work in September, 1939

The same hall one year later

The prisoner information bureau of each nation was also expected to forward those same lists to the prisoners' protecting powers, and those powers too would send them on to the prisoners' own governments. This provided two chances— one through the Central Agency of the ICRC, one through the protecting power—for news of each captured prisoner to get back to his government and eventually to his family.

A third and more direct channel of information between prisoners and their families was also provided by the Conventions. It gave every prisoner the right to mail home a "capture card" soon after his arrival at a prison camp, and to mail postage-free cards and letters at certain intervals from then on. A "capture card" was just what it sounds like: a card signed by the prisoner, intended to inform his family that he had been captured and in which prison camp he was being held.

If the family of every prisoner had received a capture card, followed by official verifying notification from the government, and then by regular cards and letters, the work of the Central Agency might have been as simple in reality as it seemed in theory. For many reasons it proved instead to be both vast and complicated.

First of all, the prisoner-information bureaus set up by the various belligerent nations did not always work well or quickly, even if those in charge were efficient and well-meaning. When invading German forces conquered France in the spring of 1940, for example, and captured almost 2 million French soldiers, the German bureau immediately began to collect lists of the prisoners as they were assigned to various camps, and to forward those lists to the Central Agency. But the job of interviewing and listing all those men was so enormous that it was not finished for ten months. In the meantime, in those overcrowded camps, not all prisoners were quickly supplied with capture cards; and many such cards, even after they were distributed and filled out, failed to reach families driven from their homes during the German advance.

Thousands of French families, therefore, were left for long agonizing weeks without news of a son, husband or father. In search of some word as to whether a certain soldier had been wounded, killed or captured, many of those families turned to the Central Agency. That single military action, like every other major event of the war, flooded the Agency with frantic queries.

Mail also poured into the Agency from people who regarded it as a forwarding office. Thousands of prisoners and their families were convinced that their letters would be delivered more quickly and surely through the Agency than if they were mailed directly to their destinations. In many cases the Agency was indeed the only neutral center through which people could be fairly sure of reaching each other.

These complicating factors were only two of the many which forced the Agency to expand rapidly. It began as a handful of volunteers working at improvised tables in a corner of Geneva's Palace of the General Council. By the war's end its staff numbered 2,585, of whom 1,676 were volunteers giving as much time as they could; some spent all day every day at the Agency; others were able to contribute only their evening hours after their own day's work was done. Quickly that growing staff filled the big Palace and then overflowed into other buildings in Geneva. Eventually it occupied three acres of floor space in the city, including a museum, a bank and several apartments, and had extended into twenty-seven other Swiss cities, wherever space could be found.

The Agency also had to acquire the equipment and the experts without which its work would have been imposssible. Its photostat department made quick and accurate copies of lengthy prisoner lists that might run to thousands of pages. Its photographic enlarging equipment made legible those lists that arrived on microfilm. Its data-processing machines, lent by Thomas J. Watson, president of the International Business Machines Company, included time-saving card-punchers, sorters and tabulating machines.

All of that equipment, and the services of most of the staff members, were utilized to maintain the Agency's monster file of prisoners, a file which eventually held the almost incredible total of 35 million cards. That file was the means by which the Agency kept alive the contacts between millions of prisoners and their families.

Every available source of information was used to keep the file as up-to-date as possible. When a list of prisoners reached the Agency from a capturing power, that list was not forwarded to its destination until every name on it had been transferred to an individual file card, along with the rest of the information usually obtainable from such a list: the prisoner's rank, the names of his parents, his home address, his serial number, his regiment, his prisoner-of-war number, the name or number of the camp where he was held, and his physical condition—whether he was wounded, sick, or in good health.

The Agency also obtained information from its own "capture cards." These were duplicates of the official cards sent to prisoners' next of kin, but sent directly to Geneva under agreements between the Agency and the capturing powers. Sometimes those special capture cards contained the only information about a prisoner that reached the outside world.

Letters between prisoners and their families were still other sources of information for the file. A prisoner writing to his family might mention, for example, the name of a friend whom he had met in camp; that reference might make possible a new card in the file under the friend's name.

The file was divided into sections, by countries—Polish, French, German, English and so on. Staff members assigned to a section had to be able to read and write that language. They also had to be meticulously careful, because a mistake on their part could cause untold anguish—could result, for example, in a family's being told of a son's death when in fact he was still alive in a prison camp.

Every query that came into the Agency had to be handled individually. A single one might demand hours—or days or weeks—of work.

Take, for example, one of the thousands of letters that arrived on a certain day in a large sack of mail from France. It was from a mother who had not heard from her son in months, and hoped the Agency could tell her where and how he was. She said her son's name was Jean Martin.

This letter received an immediate reply. It was not, however, an answer to the mother's query. It was a request for more information. Martin is a common surname in France; the Agency file held 30,000 cards bearing that name, of which 2,000 were for men whose first name was Jean. So it was necessary to obtain from the mother more data about her son, before the Agency could let her know whether it possessed any knowledge of the one Jean Martin she was interested in.

There were 30,000 cards for French prisoners with the name of Martin

The French section of the file was not the only one in which problems arose because of many cards bearing similar names. The English section contained thousands of Smiths, hundreds of whom shared the first name of John. Smiths, and Browns too, were numerous in the American section. Schmidts and Meyers crowded the German section of the files.

Other kinds of problems arose every day because of the carelessness or ignorance of clerks making up the prisoner lists that were sent to the Agency. An Italian prison-camp clerk might make a dozen errors in a list of just twelve Greek prisoners, simply because he wrote down each man's name the way it sounded to him. A Greek prisoner's name might be Koutsoumbis; but the Greek's pronunciation of it, to the Italian's ears, would sound like Cuciumpis—and that is the way the prisoner's name would appear on the list. Consequently that name would be filed among the C's, in the Agency's Greek section; and a letter asking about a soldier named Koutsoumbis would give an Agency staff member long hours of work, and might never bring a satisfactory reply.

Arabic names gave rise to innumerable difficulties because they so frequently have variations. The name Amara, for one, may take such forms as Amari, Amairi, Hamar, Laamar, Omari and many others. An Arab prisoner himself might vary the spelling of his name on different occasions. His relatives might be equally inconsistent when they wrote him, or queried the Agency about him. Many an Agency staff member had more than one baffling experience with an Arab family sending dozens of letters inquiring about the fate of a son—and spelling the son's name differently in each letter.

No one could go on working at the Agency for even a single week who did not have enormous patience, a high degree of intelligence, and the feeling that every one of those thousands of file cards represented a vital link between a despairing family and a soldier cut off from them by barbed wire and enemy guards. To maintain those links Agency staff members handled each card as carefully as if it were a human life. They worked tirelessly to make their files as great a source of help as it was possible for them to be.

They used specially colored cards, for example, to cross-reference each name under all the forms in which it might be written. The Hungarian name Szabo, they knew, might sound to clerks of various nationalities as if it were spelled Sabo, Sabau or Sabu; therefore the name had cross-reference cards under all those spellings. This meant that if a query arrived about a soldier named Szabo, the staff searcher might have to look at four separate places in the Hungarian section in order to find the name he was seeking. The name Johnson was also cross-referenced, as Johnston, Johnstone, Jonson, Jonnson and Jonsson, just to make sure that a particular prisoner's file card could be found, no matter how his name had been spelled in a prison clerk's report.

Many Swiss are proficient linguists, living as they do in the heart of Europe and hearing several languages in the course of their daily lives. The Agency had little difficulty, therefore, enlisting staff members able to read and write French, German, English, Spanish, Italian, Polish, Dutch, Finnish, Greek and other European tongues. It could not so readily find men or women able to handle file cards and answer letters written in Arabic, in the varying languages of India, in numerous African dialects. But somehow, somewhere, the Agency always found a person able to understand and make himself understood in every one of the tongues represented by the half-hundred nations taking part in the war.

When no card could be found to match a query about a certain man, the Agency did not simply give up and report that fact to an anxious inquirer. Instead it took a series of time-consuming steps.

First a staff member, armed with data on the man's unit, or regiment, checked to determine if any information on that unit had recently arrived at the Agency and was still being processed.

If this effort proved fruitless, an inquiry was sent out to the information bureau of the government presumably holding the soldier prisoner; at the same time another similar inquiry might go to the Red Cross Society of that country, asking it to institute a search for the man.

Or, if other soldiers of the man's own unit could be discovered in some prison camp, those soldiers would be queried and asked to give any information they might possess about the man whose whereabouts were still unknown.

Most of such efforts were eventually successful. The Agency might discover that a "lost" man had been shifted from one camp to another, where the commandant had failed to issue him a capture card. Or it might trace him to a hospital where he had lain for weeks, unconscious and unable to give his name. Or the investigation might turn up the grim fact of his death.

Sometimes the Agency was asked to search not for one "lost" man, but for thousands. This happened after the fall of France early in the war.

A French force of 1,700,000 had been defeated by the German invaders. The dead, hospitalized and captured among them, as finally reported to the Agency at the end of ten months, numbered 1,660,000. That figure left 40,000 French soldiers still unaccounted for.

Most of those men, it seemed likely, had been killed during the swift French retreat, and buried where they fell in unmarked graves. But it was always possible that several thousand had somehow escaped, or been captured and somehow overlooked by the prison clerks. And for legal reasons alone even the deaths had to be authenticated if possible, so that official reports could be made to families who might be in desperate need of the sums due soldiers' survivors.

The Agency therefore undertook, on behalf of those 40,000 men, what it called a Regimental Inquiry. This was a method of search which involved questioning all known prisoners who might possess information about even a single one of the missing soldiers.

The vast job was done with the help of the IBM sorting and tabulating machines. It could scarcely have been completed without them.

First the 40,000 names had to be divided according to the military units in which the men had served—regiments, battalions, companies and platoons. Then every one of the 1,660,000 French prisoner cards already in the file had to be run through sorting machines, to locate the soldiers who had served in the missing men's units. That search brought forth 570,000 names, each one of a man who had served in the unit of at least one of the "lost" soldiers. The job of printing those names, with the help of the Agency's four tabulating machines, required thirty hours of continuous operation. Then letters had to go out to all 570,000 men, along with special reply forms and envelopes for mailing the forms back to Geneva.

Those letters brought 150,000 replies. Most of them contained the careful recollection of a prisoner who had seen a comrade fall, who had perhaps even remained with him as he died and knew where he was buried. Some included detailed descriptions, and even crudely drawn maps, that later led grieving families straight to unmarked graves, and enabled them to bring bodies home for reburial if they wished.

Altogether that particular Regimental Inquiry solved the mystery behind three out of ever four of those 40,000 names.

Another kind of mystery the Central Agency was often asked to solve was the identity of a body whose only identifying papers were too dirty or bloodstained or charred to be legible. When such a body was found on a battlefield, the officer in charge customarily gathered up the man's belongings, put them into an envelope, and sent them to Geneva. There they were turned over to a chemist who worked with such meager equipment as an ultraviolet lamp, chemical reagents, and a few sheets of colored cellophane that served as filters. During the course of the war that chemist patiently studied some 90,000 collections of objects—identity cards, letters, notebooks and so forth—and managed to identify the owners of all but a scant thousand of them.

Two subdivisions of the Central Agency had highly specialized tasks. One was its Medical Section. The other was its Civilian Message Center.

The Medical Section kept a close watch on that small but important group of captured military men listed as medical personnel. The Geneva Conventions required that these men be immediately sent back to their own country, unless their services were required to care for the sick and wounded among their fellow prisoners. But the Conventions were often ignored in the stress of wartime. The Medical Section therefore sought the release of many doctors, orderlies and nurses illegally kept behind prison walls.

Often a Section delegate had to undertake an elaborate search, with the help of National Red Cross Societies, before he could locate a captured man whose release he hoped to secure. Often, too, he found a medical officer lacking the credentials necessary to prove he was eligible for repatriation —lacking them because his medical papers had been lost, or because they had been illegally taken from him after capture. Obtaining duplicate credentials in those cases was a job that demanded patience; so was the job of convincing stubborn authorities that the new credentials were valid. Such negotiations could drag on for months, slowed by war-disrupted communication channels and by prison officials determined not to release men in their charge.

The Agency's Medical Section also tried to track down prisoners so sick or seriously wounded that they were, according to the Geneva Conventions, eligible for exchange. Each prison camp commandant was responsible for sending a list of such prisoners to the Medical Section. Many never did so. Often the presence of an invalid in a certain camp was known only through letters he or a friend wrote home, or sent directly to the Agency.

Finding such a man was, once more, merely the first step in a lengthy process. The next step in this case involved requesting the prison camp's own medical staff, or an impartial medical commission, to report on the prisoner's condition. If that diagnosis indicated the prisoner was eligible for exchange, the Agency made a formal application for his repatriation. If it was granted—and often it was not—the prisoner's name was added to the list of those already approved for repatriation, since exchange of prisoners took place by groups rather than individually.

Then transportation had to be scheduled, after securing the agreement of both belligerents as to the route that would be followed. Even at that point, when all seemed ready for the prisoner's return to his homeland, a sudden change of mind on the part of one belligerent could make it necessary to reopen the whole series of negotiations.

Negotiations for exchanging British and German sick and wounded prisoners, begun in July 1940, went on for more than three years. Not until October 1943 did the first exchanges actually take place.

In the meantime the Medical Section had been doing what it could to alleviate the suffering of the imprisoned sick and wounded. Those held in German camps were particularly badly off for lack of dental care, artificial limbs, eyeglasses, vitamins and medicines. Appeals to Germany to remedy their state brought the reply that the needed supplies could not be obtained because Germany's enemies were blockading her ports. This was known to be true. Food in Germany was

*An exchange of British and German prisoners; the two civilians are
ICRC delegates representing Germany and England, respectively*

*British and Italian prisoners are exchanged in Izmir; the stretcher-
bearers are members of the Turkish Red Crescent Society*

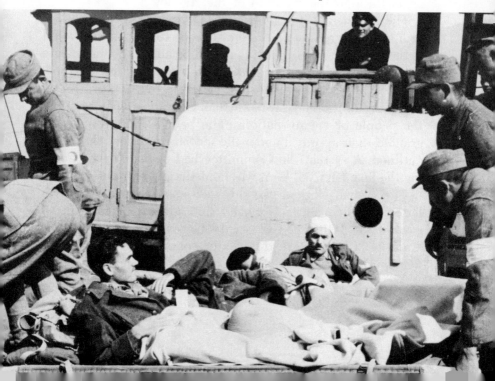

already so scarce that thousands of war prisoners detained inside the country were kept alive only by the relief parcels delivered to them by the Red Cross. The Agency therefore undertook to furnish the supplies itself.

Using funds from National Red Cross Societies, and from Swiss citizens, the Agency set up more than sixty dental clinics in German prison camps. A workroom in Switzerland accepted contributions of discarded dental plates, and its staff salvaged nearly 200,000 artificial teeth which were used to make dentures for prisoners.

The Agency also collected old eyeglasses, sorted them and salvaged them for re-use. Some 25,000 pairs of those glasses went to Allied prisoners in German camps.

Artificial arms and legs, bought from Swiss factories with contributed funds, and fitted by Swiss experts, helped crippled prisoners to get around, or perhaps to feed themselves.

Literally tons of medicines and vitamins, contributed by Red Cross Societies, were supplied to sick and wounded prisoners through the medium of the Agency.

The Civilian Message Center, originally started with a staff of four, grew to an organization of 150 persons devoted to the idea that human beings should be able to communicate with each other about personal matters even during wartime.

The ICRC sought permission to set up the Center as soon as the declaration of war banned all correspondence between the people of enemy nations. The belligerent governments granted their approval under the special conditions the ICRC outlined. A system the Committee had devised earlier, during the Spanish Civil War, was immediately put into practice.

The system worked like this: a Frenchman, say, wrote a letter to his cousin in Germany, and addressed it to him in care of the ICRC in Geneva. In Geneva a member of the Message Center staff read the letter, condensed it into twenty-five words or less of purely personal news or queries, copied the condensed version on a special letter form, and then sent the form on to the German addressee. Military censors could read such letters quickly, if they wished. Usually they passed them without reading. The ICRC had guaranteed that its staff would transmit no information of a military nature, and the ICRC was known to keep its word.

When the civilian mail reaching the Message Center increased enormously, as more and more countries entered the war, a new method became necessary. Once more the approval of the belligerent governments had to be obtained. Then the special letter forms the Center staff had been using could be used directly by people wishing to send mail through the Agency. They could get such forms through their Red Cross Society, and give that Society their letter for posting to Geneva.

From then on, in Geneva, the Message Center staff had only to read each twenty-five-word letter, to make sure it contained no military information, and send it on to its destination—although most of these letters were also checked as possible sources of information for the prisoner-of-war files. Each National Red Cross Society was also responsible for delivering the messages sent to persons in its own country.

The Center processed and forwarded a total of 24 million civilian messages during the war, or 10,000 letters on an average day. But there were few "average" days during the conflict. Each time a major military offensive uprooted thousands of families, or separated members of the same family, whole new groups of people became eager to get in touch with friends or relatives from whom they had been cut off. That is why the Center was sometimes deluged by a torrent of 80,000 letters in a single twenty-four-hour period.

Even during such crises, however, the staff members tried to get each letter on its way again as soon as possible. They knew how anxiously it was awaited. They also knew it might still have to travel for weeks before reaching its destination.

The mail routes the Center used, which it had to work out for itself, were often exteremely roundabout.

One example was the 1,000-mile journey a letter traveled between Rome and Naples at the time those two Italian cities—actually less than 150 miles apart—were in the control of opposing forces. A Roman letter writer's message first went north to Geneva, where it was processed before being sent to Marseilles, in the south of France, by truck. There it was transferred to an ICRC-chartered ship which carried it out through the Strait of Gibraltar into the Atlantic, and on north to Lisbon in neutral Portugal. At Lisbon the letter was picked up by an Allied military plane and flown back across the Mediterranean to Algiers. And there, once more, it was put aboard a ship and carried finally to Naples.

The war's end made very little immediate difference in the vast amount of work that had been going on for six years in the various offices of the Central Agency. Eventually the Civilian Message Center became less busy. Eventually the Medical Section completed the bulk of its work. But families went on stubbornly seeking missing soldiers; returned soldiers persistently tried to find parents, wives or children who had disappeared during the war. The Central Agency continued to be flooded with queries.

Finally reorganized under the new name of Central Tracing Agency, it continued to add cards to its files as time went on—cards of refugees, cards of stateless persons, cards of prisoners taken during the conflicts of the late 1940's, the 1950's, the 1960's. Fifteen years after the War was over it was still receiving queries at the rate of some 50,000 a year, and adding to an index that by then held over 50 million cards.

Before the War was a month old, delegates from the ICRC were making their first visits to prisoner-of-war camps. They were still making such visits when the hostilities had ceased. They made over 11,000 of them altogether.

An ICRC delegate interviews French soldiers in a German prison camp

Volunteers classify books collected by the Intellectual Relief Service

Most visits followed a regular procedure, worked out to save time and to give a delegate the best possible picture of conditions in the prisoner-of-war camp.

First, after presenting his credentials, the delegate talked privately with the camp leader, the prisoner chosen by his fellow captives to serve as their spokesman. A medical officer —also a prisoner—and a chaplain might join in the conversation. The delegate could learn from them about the general conditions inside the camp, and whether or not swift, and perhaps temporary, improvements had been made in preparation for his expected visit. Then he started on his rounds, usually with both the camp leader and the camp commandant.

In the prisoners' sleeping quarters he noted the lighting, the ventilation, the quality and quantity of bedding, the presence or absence of fire-prevention equipment. In the kitchen and mess halls he checked for cleanliness, took a sample of the drinking water for later testing, and studied the amount and variety of daily rations served.

He found out exactly how many items of clothing each prisoner received. He learned how prisoners obtained admission to the sick ward, and what kind of treatment they received there. He made a count of the seriously ill, of those with contagious diseases, of those with ailments caused by dietary deficiencies. He went over the camp's death records.

He studied the prisoners' working conditions, which were regulated by the Geneva Conventions: prisoners had to be paid for work they were required to do, and could not be forced to perform hazardous, injurious, or degrading labor.

He studied the conditions under which the prisoners spent their leisure time. He inquired, for example, about the space available to them for recreation. He checked to see whether they had writing materials, sports equipment, and a variety of books including the texts some prisoners used for continuing their education during confinement.

He asked if there was a complaint book in which prisoners could register their grievances. He inquired about disciplinary measures taken against inmates who broke camp regulations. He made certain that prisoners were able to learn about their rights from an openly posted copy of the Prisoners of War Code, to which all signers of the Geneva Conventions subscribed.

Finally the delegate met privately with the prisoners' spokesman, and with individual prisoners who wished to talk with him about their needs and wants. One man might request a pair of glasses. Another might ask the delegate to try to obtain news of his family, from whom he had not heard in months. Still another might report mistreatment at the hands of a prison guard.

Sometimes, before a visit was over—and it might last for several days in a large camp—certain minor problems might already be solved. If the commandant of the camp was capable and conscientious, he might agree on the spot to make the changes which the delegate recommended as the result of what he had seen and heard. Serious violations of the Prisoners of War Code might have to be taken up later with a higher authority. In any case the delegate later made a full, accurate and impartial report of his visit. It covered everything he had learned, any changes the commandant had agreed to put into effect, and any additional changes the delegate himself advised.

One such report might originally be written in German, by a German-speaking Swiss who had visited a German camp for British prisoners. Another might be written in English, by an English-speaking delegate who had visited a British camp for German prisoners. But all reports were eventually translated into French, and identical copies of the translation were sent to the government of the prisoners' homeland, and to the detaining power—that is, to the power holding the soldiers captive. The reason for sending the French version to both governments was to guarantee that each received exactly the same report, down to the last syllable. This prevented the disagreements that sometimes arise over the meaning of a word that has been translated from one language into another.

Representatives of protecting powers made camp visits too, of course, as they were authorized to do by the Geneva Conventions. They did not even have to obtain official permission for their visits, as ICRC delegates always had to do. But as more countries entered the war, the few remaining neutral nations able to serve as protecting powers could not send delegates to every camp frequently enough. Like most belligerent nations, they welcomed the work of the ICRC in this field. And without the steady rounds of visits by ICRC delegates, certain governments would not have been able to make effective official protests against unfair treatment of their own nationals—protests often backed by the implied threat of retaliation.

"We know," such a threat might say in effect, "that you are mistreating men of our armed forces whom you are holding as prisoners. If we do not learn that their condition has improved, we shall start treating your nationals in our prison camps in a similar way."

The ICRC itself never used the threat of retaliation, which is expressly forbidden by the Conventions. It did make use of the principle of reciprocity for much the same purpose. A delegate visiting English prisoners in Germany, for example, could bolster his plea for more food by telling the German authorities of the better treatment German prisoners were receiving in England.

The principle of reciprocity was of no use, however, in helping to improve conditions in closed camps—in camps, that is, which ICRC delegates were not permitted to visit. There were many of these.

The Soviet Union, for example, which had not signed the

1929 Geneva Conventions, refused to permit delegates to visit the camps where she imprisoned German captives. Germany therefore, declaring herself no longer bound to treat Russian captives according to the Conventions, also closed the camps where those men were imprisoned. Afterward it was learned that thousands of those Russians and Germans died under severe mistreatment.

Japan had not signed the Geneva Conventions either, but she had agreed in a general way to comply with them to the extent her enemies did. And the Japanese Red Cross, like National Societies everywhere, stood ready to relieve the suffering of captives wherever possible. But the official Japanese attitude toward capture had the result of closing many prisons. This attitude regarded capture as a disgrace, and a captured man as unworthy of humane treatment. A captured Japanese soldier usually asked that his name not be reported, so that his family and his government would never know what had happened to him. Japanese authorities, therefore, who did not expect good treatment for their own captured men—who did not even ask for it—could not understand why an ICRC delegate should be seeking good treatment for the prisoners Japan held. For the most part they refused permission for camp inspections, as they refused Japanese Red Cross requests to aid the inmates of those camps. Red Cross relief supplies did find their way into some camps, although by no means into all.

The ICRC's most hopeless efforts during the war were those made on behalf of the civilians in enemy-occupied countries—that vast group of people for whom humanitarian international law offered no protection whatever.

Most of those civilians lived in countries Germany had conquered outright or brought under her control. Most of them were suffering under new Nazi-inspired laws. Some of those laws permitted the seizure and imprisonment without trial of anybody who "threatened the security of Nazi Germany," a vague phrase which could mean almost anything an arresting officer wanted it to mean. Other laws permitted the confinement in ghettos, or the seizure by force, of anyone of Jewish or other non-Aryan blood.

Because of those laws thousands of men, women and even children were herded into cattle cars and shipped to slave-labor camps, or to the concentration camps whose names have become symbols of evil—Dachau, Auschwitz, Buchenwald and others. There many of them died of heat, cold, starvation or disease, of exhaustion from labor under slave conditions, of lethal gas in chambers built for mass extermination.

Persistently, patiently, the ICRC used every possible opportunity to get help to those civilian war victims. Occasionally it succeeded, usually in some area where the newly imposed laws were not fully enforced.

Working through the Rumanian Red Cross, for example, and using funds collected largely in the United States, the ICRC was responsible for keeping some 200,000 Jews alive in Rumania for the duration of the war.

Working with the embassy of neutral Sweden and the Swedish Red Cross, the ICRC set up hospitals and a first-aid station in Hungary, and the ICRC delegate there issued 30,000 "letters of protection" to men too old or too ill to do heavy work. He issued the letters on his own initiative; they had no legal force at all; but the Hungarian police respected them, for some unexplained reason, and those bits of paper thus saved all 30,000 men from being drafted into forced-labor battalions.

Contributions of food, clothing, medicine and even money could sometimes be distributed to Jews in the Balkan countries, in Greece, in unoccupied France.

German regulations made it almost impossible to help the inmates of the concentration camps, however, at least until the war was almost over and millions were already dead.

POLONAIS INTERNÉ

EXPÉDITEUR:
ABSENDER

Comité International de la Croix - Rouge

Name: *Paschke* Nr: *28308*

Vorname: *Josef* geb: *5. 12. 190*

Block: *28*

Stube: *1*

Betr.: **Z.** *...* **Deutschland**

LAGER DACHAU 3 K
bei München

Obige Adresse durchstreichen **UND WENDEN**. Dann Empfang des Pakets links bestätigen und die Etikette nach Genf zurücksenden.

Barrér l'adresse ci-dessus et accuser réception du colis **AU VERSO**, puis retourner l'étiquette à Genève.

EMPFANGSBESCHEINIGUNG
QUITTANCE

Erhalten am *25. XI 1944*
Reçu le

Unterschrift des umstehenden Empfängers:
Signature du destinataire:

Ks. Paschke Josef
Nr. 28308 Geb. 5. 12. 1906
Genaue Adresse (Nect): *28/1*
Lager: *Dachau 3K*

GEBÜHRENFREI

Zurück an das

INTERNATIONALE KOMITEE
VOM ROTEN KREUZ

ZENTRALSTELLE FÜR KRIEGSGEFANGENE

GENF
(SCHWEIZ)

Receipt for a relief package delivered to a concentration camp inmate

One of the first tiny chinks in the forbidding wall surrounding those inmates was the Germans' agreement to accept relief parcels addressed to a specific person at a specific camp. This permission was not nearly as generous as it seemed, because no capture cards were ever sent out of concentration camps, and no lists of camp inmates were ever sent to the ICRC. Even the existence of many of the camps was a closely guarded secret. In all of Germany, at the time that permission was granted, the ICRC knew the location of only sixty-some individual prisoners.

Those sixty persons, of course, were immediately sent help in the form of parcels. And when the ICRC received receipts for those parcels, each one was signed not only by the person to whom the parcel had been addressed, but by several others as well. The camp inmates were making use of those receipts to send news of their location to the outside world. The new names were added to the list of those to whom parcels might be sent. And from then on that list grew, slowly but steadily, increased every day or so by names obtained from underground sources, from escaped prisoners, from still other parcel receipts.

All through 1943 and 1944 the ICRC continued with little success to plead for better treatment for concentration camp inmates. Its requests grew more urgent as food in Germany became scarcer, since it was known that those camps were always given the least—and the worst—of the available rations. Still the ICRC made almost no progress. Then, in 1945, when the Germans realized that their defeat was inevitable and drawing ever closer, many of the ICRC's requests were granted in quick succession.

Concentration camp inmates were permitted to write to their families on Red Cross message forms sent through the Central Agency. Relief parcels were allowed into the camps in bulk, whether they could be addressed to individuals or not. A number of women and children and aged persons were offered their release provided the Red Cross arranged for their transportation.

Swiftly the ICRC took advantage of every one of those opportunities, in the hope of saving people already weakened by hunger and mistreatment.

In the meantime the Allied forces were closing in on central Germany, pushing relentlessly against their enemy's collapsing lines. Word soon reached the ICRC that certain concentration camps were being evacuated, that German officers were driving their charges on foot, across open country, just ahead of the oncoming Allied armies. Those brutal marches were killing many prisoners who had managed to survive even a long incarceration—and the ICRC was powerless to go to their rescue.

But suddenly the picture changed.

The ICRC was invited to send its representative into camps that had been closed to them all during the War.

Red Cross delegates started off without delay for every camp whose name was known. They were racing against time. They knew that a German camp commandant was likely to make one of two moves as he saw the Allied forces drawing near: either he would drive his charges into forced evacuation marches; or he and his guards would abandon them, leaving them to wander out through opened gates to starve in the ravaged countryside.

Convoys of trucks were heading for Germany at the same time, each vehicle painted white and marked with red crosses. They were carrying tons of food and medicines; they were also carrying their own fuel oil, because German supplies were already exhausted. Twenty-four hours a day the convoys moved forward, each under the direction of a Red Cross delegate, until some of them overtook long lines of prisoners, many so weak that they lay unconscious by the roadside. Those who could still move were being harried on by the German storm troopers known as SS guards. But the

A convoy of trucks with supplies for a concentration camp

guards apparently did not dare to protest when a Red Cross convoy halted a marching file, and began to hand out food.

"The distribution of parcels certainly saved many lives," one typically unemotional Red Cross report stated afterward, "but it should be recorded that the mere presence of the Committee's delegates in the midst of the columns had a double psychological effect. First, the SS guards, being under the eye of the delegates, ceased their killing. Secondly, the prisoners felt they were no longer alone, that they had someone behind them who had firmly stood up to the SS. This gave them support and helped them hold out for another few days."

One Red Cross delegate reached the notorious Dachau camp before it could be evacuated, and managed to convince the officers in charge that they should surrender formally to the Allied forces at the first opportunity. When an American column reached the area soon after that, the delegate tied a white cloth to a broomstick and walked through the camp gate accompanied by a German officer.

"Bullets were flying around us," he recorded in his report. "Shortly afterward I caught sight of an American motorized section and attracted their attention by waving the flag. I at once got in touch with the American general in command and handed the camp over to him . . ."

Another delegate, who had reached the equally infamous camp known as Mauthausen, set out in a white car marked with a red cross to meet the oncoming Americans. Suddenly he found himself face to face with an advancing armored column headed by a huge tank. He stopped his car and walked forward alone, holding a white flag. The tank flaps opened, armed American soldiers jumped out and surrounded him. Quietly he stood his ground, identifying himself and explaining his presence there. Then he asked the Americans to send tanks and some 500 men forward to disarm the prison camp guards, and take charge of the prisoners.

The American officer who decided to grant his request made one condition: the delegate himself would not only accompany the soldiers into the camp, but would have to assume personal responsibility for the safety of every soldier. The delegate agreed. Slowly he started back toward the camp at the head of a line of American tanks and GI's.

"I noted with satisfaction," he reported later, "that the anti-tank defenses had been left open, as I had ordered. . . . We followed the hairpin turns of the main road leading to the fort; the crematorium could be seen in the distance. On arriving . . . I saw that, as arranged, the swastika was down and the white flag flying . . . my plan had succeeded. . . . After a short period of disorder, due to the internees' sudden liberation, the camp again became calm . . . and 60,000 human beings were freed."

The pitiful condition of those prisoners, and of the ones

in every concentration camp finally opened during the last weeks of the War, shocked the whole world. And, because the camps had not been protected by the Geneva Conventions, many men suddenly gained a new understanding of what those Conventions could mean. Soldiers who had been imprisoned in camps that were regularly inspected, and regularly supplied with Red Cross relief parcels, were particularly aware of the difference between their experience and that of the unfortunate civilians who had been sealed away from the world for months or perhaps years.

It was true that every nation had violated the Geneva Conventions to some degree during the war. Yet each violation had been carried out in a way that actually proved the strength of public opinion supporting the Conventions.

No nation accused of mistreating a group of soldier captives, for example, admitted that by doing so it was deliberately flouting the Conventions. Instead each nation attempted to prove that the Conventions did not apply in this particular instance. It might say, as the United States once did, that the masses of Japanese soldiers who surrendered at the war's end were not real prisoners of war, but captives of a new type called Surrendered Enemy Personnel, of which there was no mention in the Geneva Conventions; therefore, the United States claimed, she felt free to withold from those Japanese certain privileges guaranteed by the Conventions to all war prisoners.

Germany offered a similar excuse for her brutal treatment of captured partisan fighters. These guerilla soldiers, refusing to put down their arms although German troops officially occupied their country, rarely wore uniforms or any emblems that proclaimed their military standing; therefore, Germany claimed, they were not soldiers at all, but simply outlaws or brigands to whom the Conventions offered no protection. In many cases German authorities summarily executed the partisans they captured.

Almost invariably, in other words, in one way or another, each nation tried to avoid blame for its behavior, without declaring itself openly opposed to the Conventions it had signed and ratified. Each nation wanted the Conventions to remain in force.

And when the war was over there was general agreement that the Conventions should be extended once more, this time to offer protection to war's civilian victims too.

The International Committee of the Red Cross, honored again by the Nobel Peace Prize in 1944, had long been working toward just such an extension. Now again it led the way in a campaign that bore fruit in 1949.

That year there came into being a new—the Fourth—Geneva Convention. It guarantees, to enemy aliens and to the civilian inhabitants of enemy-occupied countries, much the same protections the Third Convention earlier won for captured soldiers. (The first two Conventions, as they are now thought of, guarantee protection in one case to those wounded in land battles, in the other case to those wounded at sea.)

I 21	(—) 21	— の 21	٢١ أ

Interdit: Transporter troupes, armes, munitions, etc. sous le couvert de l'emblème de la Croix-Rouge.

Forbidden: Transport of troops, arms, munitions, etc, under cover of the Red Cross emblem.

禁止: 在紅十字的徽記的掩护下運輸軍隊、武器、軍需品等等。

Запрещено: перевозить войска, оружие, амуницию, и т. д. под прикрытием эмблемы Красного Креста.

禁止: 赤十字の旗にかくれて軍隊, 武器, 彈藥等の輸送をしてはならない.

ممنوع. ― نقل الجيوش والا سلحة والمعدات الحربية .. الخ، بالتستروراء شارة الهلال / الصليب الاحمر.

Prohibido: Transportar tropas, armas, municiones, etc., bajo el amparo del emblema de la Cruz Roja.

Verboten: Transport von Truppen, Waffen, Munition usw. unter dem Schutz des Rotkreuz-Abzeichens.

Epekisami: Bomemi basoda baye bazoki te, mandoki, masasi na biloko binso bia etumba na bimemeli bia Croix-Rouge.

The rules of the Fourth Geneva Convention are printed in nine languages

The Fourth Geneva Convention, along with newly revised versions of the first three, was signed and ratified by governments already joining together in a United Nations.

Once more, at the end of a long and disastrous war, mankind was trying to plan for peace. Once more countries in almost every part of the globe were pledging themselves to seek new roads toward international security.

There were those who said the United Nations could not last, offering as proof the fact that the earlier League of Nations had broken down under the impact of a second World War.

There were others who pointed out that it might last, if enough men wanted it to last; and they offered as proof the fact that the Red Cross was still enduring after almost a century, although its member nations included all those in the UN and others besides—the People's Republic of China for one, neutral Switzerland for another.

Since its founding the Red Cross had proved, over and over again, that people are willing to help people even across national boundaries; that men can learn to treat all men as brothers, even their enemies.

The program of the Red Cross had foreshadowed much of what the UN would now try to accomplish. But, as the member nations of the UN themselves agreed, this did not mean the Red Cross no longer had a role to play.

Governments had long before assumed duties for which the Red Cross had once volunteered—the manning of military hospitals, for example. When that happened the Red Cross had found new work to do, had pioneered in new fields.

Now, with the UN ready to assume other tasks the Red Cross had taken upon itself, in the area of public health and welfare, for example, the Red Cross would be able to pioneer still farther ahead.

At a time when many other international organizations were being absorbed into the UN, the Red Cross, still an independent and private institution, was accepting a mandate from that newer organization to broaden and amplify its humanitarian work. Still heavily burdened by the long aftermath of World War II, it was looking ahead into a world where that war's echoes continued to sound, a world where even peace had its problems. It expected to find plenty to do.

8. Crisis in Hungary

Red Cross workers all over the world follow the news closely. They may, at any moment, hear of people somewhere in need of help.

The first report of a tornado sweeping through a certain town serves as an automatic signal sending all Red Cross emergency units in the vicinity straight to the scene of the disaster.

The report that fighting has suddenly broken out some-where—that civilians are rioting in the streets, and armed forces are firing on crowds—automatically brings local Red Cross ambulances and medical teams to the spot. When a report of that kind reached Managua, in Guatemala, in 1959, the Red Cross there later issued the following statement:

"On July 23rd, a students' demonstration, which took place at Ciudad de León, was broken up by the National Guard using firearms which caused five deaths and some fifty wounded. As soon as this news became known, a convoy left for Ciudad de León, fifty-five miles distant from Managua, and took with it all the necessary supplies to enable medico-surgical treatment to be given to the students . . ."

In the case of a tornado, or some other natural disaster, Red Cross people in other countries also go on the alert. They take it for granted that their help will be wanted if the local Red Cross and other agencies cannot cope with the problem. In the case of an outbreak of fighting, however, they have no way of knowing whether their help will be wanted or not, however many casualties may occur.

Only the International Committee can traditionally offer its services to both sides in what the Geneva Conventions describe as an "internal disturbance." National Red Cross Societies, lacking the Committee's neutrality, can carry their help across national boundaries only when they are invited to do so. The invitation is not always issued, even when the need for help is great.

A dramatic example of how the Red Cross reacts to news of an internal disturbance occurred late in October 1956. Fighting had broken out in Hungary on Tuesday, October 23rd. Civilians revolting against the government were joined by soldiers of the Hungarian Army; Soviet Russian troops and tanks were battling the Freedom Fighters, as they called themselves.

At the first fragmentary reports over the air waves, both the League and the International Committee offices in Geneva went on the alert. While the news from the Hungarian capital, Budapest, continued to be fragmentary and inconclusive, League and Committee officials tried to establish direct contact with the Hungarian Red Cross. They wanted to know if help was needed, and if foreign assistance would be permitted in the country.

All their attempts were fruitless. Telephone communication with Hungary had apparently broken down or been cut off. It was a time of tension—"unusual," one League account reported later, "even for an organization accustomed to moments of high tension."

Already the League was receiving queries from National

Societies eager to assist the victims of the Hungarian up-rising. The American Red Cross had telephoned from Wash-ington to ask what aid it could give. The Federal German Red Cross called to say it had made up and equipped a medical train which stood by, ready to move across Austria into Hun-gary as soon as permission was granted for its passage. The Italian Red Cross informed the League that it had mobile clinics waiting to move into Hungary. The Norwegian and Swedish Red Cross Societies reported that planes in both their countries were loaded with relief supplies and awaiting instructions.

And then, on the morning of Saturday, October 27th, the Hungarian Red Cross sent out a radio appeal for medical as-sistance, though without specifying the kind of supplies needed.

The Swiss Shortwave Broadcasting Station, acting in re-sponse to the ICRC's request, beamed a message back to Hungary asking for further information. The broadcasts took place every hour, and the sixth one had gone out before there was a reply. It came then, unexectedly, by telephone. The Hungarian Red Cross headquarters had been heavily dam-aged, but somehow the Secretary General had managed to get through to Geneva. The supplies most urgently needed, he said, were blood plasma, blood transfusion equipment and dressings.

Word went out immediately from the League office to in-form Societies of what was wanted. From the office of the ICRC a delegate left for Vienna, close to the Austro-Hun-garian border, where a reception center for relief supplies would be set up.

The next day, Sunday, two more ICRC delegates, carrying hundreds of precious units of human plasma ready for trans-fusions, left on a chartered Swiss plane for Hungary. The Committee's neutrality, and the humanitarian principles of the Red Cross, were their only passports into a country whose borders were by then closed to most foreigners except the government's Soviet supporters. But the plane was permitted to land. The two delegates handed the plasma to Hungarian Red Cross officials waiting at the airport. Then they took off immediately for Vienna, where relief supplies were beginning to arrive by road, rail and air.

Throughout Monday, Tuesday and the early part of Wednesday only that single Committee-chartered plane was permitted to bring plasma and other desperately needed medicines across the border. When a food shortage developed in Budapest, because of a general strike, the plane added powdered milk and other baby foods to its cargo. On Wednesday evening, as the plane came in over the Budapest airport for the sixth time, signals from the ground refused it permission to land. It was forced to turn back toward the Austrian border. For twelve hours the border remained tightly closed to traffic of all kinds.

On Thursday the anti-Soviet forces appeared to be gaining. Soviet troops were reported to be withdrawing from the country, and it was said that a new government satisfactory to the Freedom Fighters was being set up. Border regulations relaxed. Under supervision of the ICRC, a German relief train entered the country. So did several truck convoys, bearing food and other urgently needed supplies donated by various National Societies.

But suddenly the Soviet forces opened a powerful new attack on Budapest and other strongholds of the Freedom Fighters. Soviet tanks poured into the capital, past hastily thrown up barricades made of paving blocks, furniture and any other objects that could be dragged into the streets. The toll of dead and injured mounted swiftly. And no more relief supplies could get through. Once more the borders had been closed. Reports to the outside world, from the rapidly diminishing number of Freedom Fighter radio stations, told of hospitals being fired on and Red Cross workers shot down as they tried to pick up the wounded lying in the streets.

The ICRC had been broadcasting regular reminders to both forces to obey the Geneva Conventions. Hungary had ratified them as a nation. The national committee set up by the Freedom Fighters had agreed to abide by them too. But now, in response to a request from the Hungarian Red Cross —a request made in one of the last telephone calls that reached Geneva from Budapest—the ICRC made another "solemn appeal" to the belligerents through the Swiss Short-wave Service.

"The International Committee of the Red Cross is informed," the broadcast stated, "that combats are still raging in Budapest, and that numerous wounded have not yet been collected and cared for. It makes an urgent appeal to commanders and combatants to call a truce by mutual agreement in order that the wounded may be collected and evacuated. The present appeal is made by the ICRC in accordance with the provisions of Article 15 of the Fourth Geneva Convention."

The Committee's efforts to bring about a truce failed. But after five days of fierce fighting, during which Soviet forces slowly broke the resistance of the poorly armed population, the ICRC decided to challenge the closed Hungarian border. It notified the Hungarian and Soviet authorities that a convoy of fifteen trucks carrying relief supplies was leaving Vienna, and requested permission for its passage into Hungary.

The convoy reached the border the next day. The Committee delegates traveling with it began negotiations at once. All that day and all the next day they pleaded their case before the authorities, while the truck drivers waited in the cold November air.

The Soviet Union, and the powers friendly to it, had not joined the contributing nations whose gifts of food, medicines and other articles filled those trucks. The gifts had come from people sympathetic to the fighters who had challenged Soviet power. From a political point of view, therefore, the gifts were unwelcome to border guards loyal to the Soviet Union. But the delegates of the ICRC refused, as always, to talk in political terms. They took no side in the conflict. Their only purpose was to feed the hungry and to aid the injured. They urged the admission of the trucks into Hungary on purely humanitarian grounds. Finally they won their point.

Shortly before midnight, at the end of the second day, the border barriers opened. The convoy of white vehicles, all marked with the Red Cross, moved through. The ICRC delegates went with it. They alone were responsible for handing over to a newly organized Hungarian Red Cross the life-saving supplies the trucks carried.

From then on convoys of Red Cross trucks crossed the border in a steady stream. Rail and river barge routes were later opened to the Red Cross too. Trucks, trains and barges together delivered into Hungary the 35 million pounds of supplies used in a 19-million-dollar relief program.

Trucks with supplies for the victims of the Hungarian conflict cross the Austro-Hungarian border.

A fantastic amount of skillful organization was necessary to get those supplies into the hands of the million needy Hungarians the Red Cross aided in the aftermath of the fighting. Nearly 700 people worked at the task. Many of them were Swiss experts—in transport, in nutrition and other fields —placed at the ICRC's disposal by their employers. Special funds donated by National Societies paid for the upkeep of supply depots and warehouses.

Thirty-five thousand homes had been destroyed throughout the country. Thousands more, along with schools, hospitals and other buildings, had become almost useless as a protection against icy winter winds when their windows had been shattered. A special program of supplying and installing window glass was therefore planned and carried out.

Another special program provided milk for expectant mothers and for babies. Still another meant a daily hot meal for 66,000 Budapest school children. And there were special programs—they totalled 167 in all—which provided needy people and institutions with such various items as coal, soap, beds and blankets, shoes, x-ray equipment, toys and ambulances.

But the relief program carried out inside Hungary was only part of the work the International Red Cross was doing for the victims of the country's unsuccessful revolution. The rest was being done outside the country, under League direction, for the 200,000 men, women and children who fled Hungary during or after the fighting. Some 20,000 of these refugees made their way into Yugoslavia; all the others crossed the border into Austria.

In the beginning no one guessed how many people would eventually leave Hungary. The first few weary refugees who slipped over the Austrian border, found no one ready to receive them. They had arrived with little more than the clothes on their backs, and perhaps a few possessions they had been able to pile into a baby carriage or a child's wagon. They had

Hungarian refugees on their way to a railway station in Yugoslavia

Austrian villagers serve soup to the refugees

walked for a long distance in most cases. They were hungry and cold. Some of them were ill or had been wounded.

Friendly villagers along the Austrian border did what they could for them. The Austrian government offered to find them temporary accomodations. The Austrian Red Cross agreed to be responsible for their welfare. The ICRC delegates and the League representative in charge of supplies awaiting shipment into Hungary agreed to use some of those supplies for the refugees. All arrangements were haphazard and on an emergency basis; the fleeing Hungarians presented problems that had not been anticipated.

Then the trickle of refugees swelled to a torrent. Large-scale plans had to be made as quickly as possible. Within a few days the League had agreed to provide basic necessities for 10,000 Hungarians for a period of thirty days. A week later that agreement was already proving inadequate. The League then undertook to support 20,000 for sixty days. And still the refugees kept coming. For a time they were pouring over the border at the rate of 6,000 a day.

No border village could accommodate each day's new arrivals even for a single night. The refugees had to be taken immediately to one of the centers the Austrian government was opening as swiftly as possible in various parts of the country. It used any building available, whether it was suitable or not—an army barracks, a hotel, an uninhabited castle.

The new refugee centers were originally supervised by anyone who could take over the task at short notice, an Austrian Red Cross volunteer, or the delegate of some National Society who had come to Austria to superintend the distribution of supplies his organization had contributed for Hungarian relief. An American disaster-relief expert suggested the permanent plan that was soon being put into operation.

Each center was to be directed by a team of experts. Each team would consist of a leader and an administrative assistant, and specialists in the various fields under which Red

Cross work is organized: nursing, welfare, food, housing and clothing. National Societies were invited to organize such teams and send them to Austria immediately.

More than a dozen Societies responded, including the Austrian Red Cross which put seven teams to work in seven separate centers. Six teams arrived from Germany, five each from Denmark and the United States, three each from England, Canada, Sweden and Switzerland. Finland, France, the Netherlands and Norway all sent two teams. Monaco sent one. Some of those countries, along with Belgium and Liechtenstein as well, sent other volunteers to help out wherever

Refugees at Camp de Eisenstadt in Austria

they might be needed. Working under the co-ordinating plans of League experts, those Red Cross workers from four-teen separate Societies operated forty-four refugee centers in Austria. The thirty-seven centers that were set up in Yugo-slavia, most of them much smaller than the Austrian units, were all operated by the Yugoslav Red Cross, using supplies provided through the League.

In general the system worked remarkably well, in spite of the fact that the population of each camp seldom remained at the same number for two days in a row. Most of the centers grew rapidly until February, when the flow of refugees began to die down. But long before that flow had stopped, many refugees were already leaving the camps for new homes where they could take up once more their interrupted lives.

Those concerned for the refugees' future had realized from the start that few of them could find permanent homes in Austria. The majority would have to be resettled elsewhere. And so, while frantic efforts were still being made to prepare temporary quarters for the first arrivals, plans were being made to move refugees out of these quarters as soon as pos-sible.

At the telegraphed request of the UN High Commissioner for Refugees, fifteen European governments opened their doors to homeless families. The first to leave Austria went to Switzerland on Swiss Red Cross trains that had arrived in Austria loaded with relief supplies. Shortly afterward British Red Cross planes that brought in relief supplies left with refugees heading for homes in England, Ireland and Canada.

The United States agreed to accept thousands. The Hun-garians were also welcomed by many countries in South America, by Australia and New Zealand, by Rhodesia and South Africa and Israel. Almost without exception Red Cross workers met them at every step along the way to offer hot sandwiches or meals to adults and children and milk to babies, and to provide any necessities the travelers required.

When the emigrants reached their destinations they found still other Red Cross volunteers waiting with offers of help, sometimes even with the good news of homes ready for occupancy and employers ready to offer jobs.

The movement in and out of Austria—and in and out of Yugoslavia—went on for eleven months, until seven out of eight refugees were settled in new homes in other lands. A few remained in Austria; a few more remained in Yugoslavia. Still others—one out of every fifteen who had fled—eventually returned to Hungary.

In the meantime each camp, in spite of its shifting population, was developing a kind of spirit of its own. Probably many of the refugees felt that spirit first at Christmastime, when children in every camp in Austria received a gift coupon which they could take to a shop and exchange for a full outfit of winter clothes—clothes they could pick out for themselves. The gift coupons had been bought out of funds contributed by the Red Cross Juniors of four continents. Then a

Gift boxes from Juniors around the world

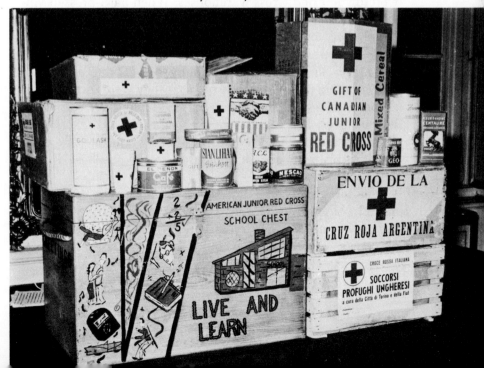

toy caravan arrived at every camp, and distributed toys from the Juniors of Federal Germany, the Netherlands and the United States. And gay pictures and posters went up on the camp walls, sent by the Juniors of Belgium, Canada, Denmark and Turkey.

By the first of the year Red Cross Juniors were also supplying all the camps with a wonderful variety of things that made living easier and pleasanter even in the dreariest barracks. American young people provided washing machines and sewing machines, and chests of school materials. More school materials came from Belgium. Paints and brushes came from Denmark. There were games from India, sewing materials from Sweden, footballs and team uniforms from England. Phonographs and records, basketballs and other sports equipment were bought with funds that had been collected by the children of Australia, Canada, Lebanon, New Zealand and Thailand.

Not all the gifts that poured into the Austrian supply centers were as wisely chosen as those the Juniors sent. There were, for example, the tons of used clothes that piled up in overcrowded Red Cross warehouses. When hard-pressed volunteers found the time to open the crates in which the clothes had arrived, they often discovered a discouraging jumble of garments of all sizes for men, women and children. And when the articles were finally sorted and examined, many of them proved to be so old that they were unwearable.

The clothes had been occupying valuable space for which the Red Cross had to pay rent. Sorting them had taken valuable time. Even when they were sold as waste, they brought in only a tiny sum that could be used for the purchase of new and usable clothing.

"Sending things like this doesn't represent a very good example of 'people helping people,'" one weary volunteer said at the end of a day spent handling hundreds of threadbare coats, tattered dresses and shapeless shoes.

A relief shipment from overseas

Henry Dunant's brief description of the idea behind the Red Cross had made it sound very simple. But some of the efforts to help the Hungarian refugees, like many earlier efforts on behalf of the Red Cross, proved that "helping" is a skill which must be acquired, like any other.

Fortunately the teaching of that skill is basic to most national Red Cross programs. The members of the teams who operated the refugee camps in Austria had learned it well. They proved their ability in many ways.

A camp nutritionist, for example, knew that giving the refugees a healthful, balanced diet was only one part of her job. She also saw to it that the foods she ordered from the supply depot included paprika and the other seasonings so many Hungarians prefer. Usually she could rely on the refugees who volunteered to help in the kitchen to see to it that the food was prepared in the way their people liked best.

Letters of thanks go from Camp Klosterneuburg in Austria to Red Cross Juniors of Darien, Connecticut

There was almost no limit to the tasks the camp welfare workers took on. They organized nurseries for young children and classes for older boys and girls who were not able to attend schools near the centers. They organized classes for adults too, in sewing, music, languages and a dozen other subjects from typewriting to electronics. Sometimes refugees taught courses in the subjects that they knew; sometimes members of the camp team added teaching chores to their other duties. One American team taught English to those who hoped to make their homes eventually in an English-speaking country, while French teams taught French and German teams taught German.

The welfare workers also managed somehow to obtain tools for many of the skilled professional men and craftsmen among the camp residents. Soon refugee carpenters were building playground equipment for the camp nurseries, and remodeling drafty buildings into snug classrooms and recreational halls. Hungarian artists and mural painters decorated those rooms. Skilled seamstresses made curtains for them on the sewing machines the Juniors had contributed.

During the winter months the welfare workers rounded up odds and ends of material that could be transformed into costumes and curtains for the plays and dances and concerts the campers staged. The whole surrounding community often turned out for these performances, or to look at exhibits of the refugees' art work, embroidery or ceramics.

In the spring there were outdoor sports. One American team introduced horseshoe-pitching in its camp; another introduced baseball. Members of a German team taught archery. Camp teams challenged each other, or challenged teams made up of Austrians living in the neighborhood. And one Swiss team, in charge of a Vienna center which had no space for outdoor activities, planned visits for the refugees to Schönbrunn Palace and various other historic spots in and near the city.

Many churches and charitable organizations sent help to the refugees. The UN contributed funds, as did many national governments. But the bulk of the supplies used in all the refugee centers in Austria and Yugoslavia were contributed by fifty-two National Red Cross Societies and Junior Sections, and were distributed by League supervisors.

The relief program that had started in October 1956, when that first news bulletin reached Geneva from the Hungarian Red Cross, went on for eight months in Hungary itself, for eleven months in Austria and Yugoslavia, and for much longer than that in the many lands where Red Cross people helped the Hungarian emigrants to build new lives for themselves. The action set in motion by that bulletin proved to be the largest relief program undertaken with Red Cross resources between the founding of the Red Cross and its hundredth birthday.

9. *"All Are Brothers"*

Before the Red Cross reached its hundredth birthday in 1963, it had become an accepted part of daily life all around the world. Today the reports of its many activities fill dozens of pages in the bulletins, journals and other publications it brings out every year. Newspapers often carry headlined stories of Red Cross achievements. Even oftener its work is taken so completely for granted that it receives no public mention at all.

If a medal is given to a lifeguard who rescues a drowning child, for example, even the donors of the medal may not know that the rescuer learned his life-saving and resuscitation techniques in Red Cross first-aid and water-safety courses.

If an auto racer's car overturns on a curve, and the injured man is quickly and competently treated at the edge of the track, the anxious onlookers are seldom aware that the driver will owe his life to a Red Cross team trained to aid accident victims.

The safety programs so common in industry today have been planned with Red Cross help, though the workers who benefit from them are not always aware of it.

School hygiene courses often rely on materials the Red Cross has prepared, whether the students in those courses realize it or not.

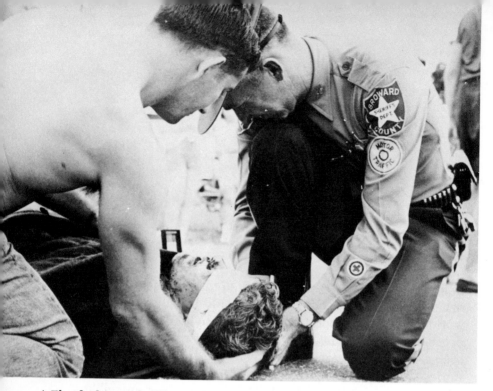

A Florida deputy sheriff gives first aid to an injured motorist

Youngsters learn to swim in the Red Cross water-safety program

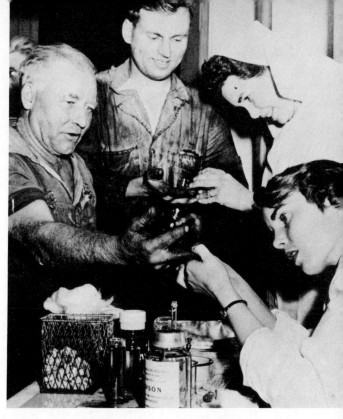

Donors give blood to the Red Cross at a railway shop in western Canada

A class for nurses in São Paulo, Brazil

Doctors and nurses themselves, though they may attend Red Cross medical meetings and conferences, do not always know how many medical advances have been made through Red Cross initiative or with Red Cross co-operation. To mention a single example: the blood derivative, fibrinogen, widely used to control hemorrhages, was first isolated by scientists working with the Red Cross blood donors program during World War II.

In most communities the Red Cross is, of course, only one of several publicly supported organizations which usually co-operate in many ways. Red Cross leaders are often leaders in some of those other organizations too, and this makes it easier for them to weave Red Cross programs into community-wide efforts for helping those who need help, for improving health standards, for promoting a better understanding among all people.

This fact—that the Red Cross leaders tend to be widely active and respected in their communities—has been true since the earliest days of the Committee of Five in Geneva. That Committee's members could speak to the Swiss government authorities as friends and equals, and could thus persuade them to call the conference that gave birth to the first Geneva Convention.

In Geneva today this same kind of friendliness and equality exists between people in the ICRC and League office, and officials of the Swiss government. Today, perhaps even more importantly, those two Red Cross offices are also closely linked with the Geneva office of the United Nations and the Geneva headquarters of WHO, the World Health Organization.

There are formal, officially recognized relations among the four offices. But their closest ties are their mutual goals and purposes. The ICRC and the UN have co-operated for the protection of civilians in countries torn by internal conflict, and on refugee aid programs. The League and the WHO work together on world-wide programs to fight tuberculosis and poliomyelitis, to prevent accidents, to improve child and maternal welfare. The Red Cross agrees fully with the peaceful purposes of the UN, and with the WHO's aim to bring to all mankind the health it defines as "a state of complete physical, mental and social well-being."

When WHO authorities became aware of the numbers of poisoned paralysis victims in Morocco in 1959, they didn't hesitate to join the Moroccan Red Crescent Society in seeking Red Cross aid for them. They called on the Red Cross just as unhesitatingly when they recognized the need for a unique medical program in the Congo in 1960.

That program was actually nothing more than an extension of the kind of work the Red Cross does daily in many parts of the world. The circumstances surrounding it were so dramatic, however, that it earned Red Cross volunteers the public attention they often deserve but less often receive.

The story of that program began almost immediately after the Congo achieved national independence on June 30, 1960.

Belgium had been ruling the sprawling equatorial Congo for seventy-five years, and during that time had done very little to train its population of 13½ million Congolese for positions of responsibility. The 100,000 European residents of the country ran almost every aspect of its industry, business, government and technical services. Under Belgian control Congolese had been permitted to become "medical assistants" in hospitals, for example, but none had been trained as doctors. In 1960 all of the 760 physicians and surgeons in the land were Europeans.

Riots among the Congolese in 1959 had convinced Belgium that she could no longer hold the country as a colonial possession. Her abrupt offer of independence was accepted by leaders who had slight experience of leadership. Further riots occurred as soon as independence became a fact.

Tribal enmities older than Belgian domination broke into

open warfare. Troops mutinied. Belgian property was pillaged. Belgian residents were attacked. The Europeans who quickly fled the country included the majority of its doctors, along with many nurses and technicians.

The ICRC immediately sent two delegates into the region to try to assure the safety of civilians and of neutral hospital zones.

Within less than two months the UN Security Council, fearful that the conflicts would grow into a large-scale war, voted to send a military force into the Congo in the hope of restoring order.

Weeks before the UN forces arrived, however, the government of the Congo had become so alarmed over its deteriorating health services that it sought the advice of WHO experts. These experts had visited hospitals, found them unsupervised and lacking trained personnel—and had swiftly appealed to ICRC delegates in the Congo for Red Cross help. Their first request was for ten medical teams, each willing to accept responsibility for one hospital or medical center for a period of three months.

The request was forwarded to the League office in Geneva. The League office immediately cabled various National Societies. In forty-eight hours all the requested teams had been recruited.

Two days later a team from Norway was already in Africa, and the other nine were on their way.

But during that brief interval the WHO experts, continuing their survey of the Congo, were beginning to comprehend the full extent of the emergency created there by the steady outflow of Europeans. Except in the province of Katanga, where many Belgians still remained, normal health services had completely broken down. Clinics were deserted. Hospitals were empty; many had been looted and pillaged, or damaged by shelling or fire. Patients had been abandoned. Any epidemic that broke out was almost certain to sweep unchecked to the borders of the country, and beyond.

The ICRC office in Léopoldville

An ICRC delegate supervises the distribution of milk

Once more the WHO experts conferred with the ICRC delegates, and asked for further Red Cross help.

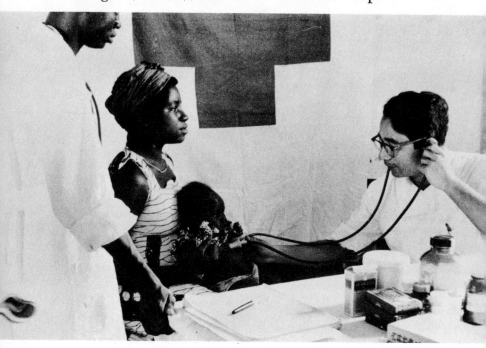

A member of the Japanese team examines a patient

The situation was difficult on many counts.

World powers were already taking sides in the dissensions among Congolese leaders. Even the UN would be regarded as a belligerent when its forces began to take action against certain Congolese elements. Under such circumstances doctors from West Germany, for example, might find themselves extremely unwelcome in certain parts of the country; doctors from Communist East Germany might be equally unwelcome in other areas. Only an organization of unquestioned neutrality, such as the ICRC, could expect to function at all in so disturbed a land.

First of all it was necessary for the League and the International Committee to sign an agreement giving the Committee control of the medical personnel the League would recruit. Under the terms of that agreement all doctors and nurses who went to serve in the Congo would, in effect, leave their own nationalities behind as they crossed the border, and enter the country as representatives of the ICRC. And the ICRC delegate who met them there would escort them to their destinations, and do everything in his power to assure their safety and protection as neutrals.

Second, there was the problem of recruiting teams from National Societies which were already carrying heavy burdens. For more than two years they had been contributing much of the relief supplies needed to keep alive more than 200,000 Algerian refugees in Morocco and Tunisia. In the first half of 1960 they had sent volunteers, as well as huge sums of money, to aid hundreds of thousands of people left homeless after disastrous earthquakes in Morocco and Chile. Red Cross volunteers from many nations were also still at work among the paralysis victims in Morocco.

Nevertheless the second request for help, forwarded to the League office by the ICRC, was promptly sent out to member Societies. It was just as promptly met. Before the Congo's independence was a month old, twenty-seven teams from twenty National Societies were on duty in the country. Some teams consisted of two nurses and a doctor with surgical training and a knowledge of tropical diseases. Others were made up of three nurses, a surgeon and a physician experienced in tropical medicine.

All of them went to work as soon as they reached the area to which they were assigned.

In Luluabourg, in the province of Kasai, a Norwegian team was soon performing almost 100 operations a month.

A team from the Iranian Red Lion and Sun Society, which operated on 434 patients in four months, still found time to treat hundreds of patients suffering from diseases and malnutrition, and to train Congolese women to serve as midwives and nurses.

Some teams found themselves working in hospitals which were well equipped. Others were less fortunate.

"In all three hospitals in which we were called upon to perform operations," a Finnish team reported, "the scissors did not cut and had crossed blades, and the forceps were of the oldest clumsy model with ill-fitting jaws. No type of modern nontraumatic surgery, the stitching of nerves and plastic work on tendons, or other fine surgery could be thought of with those instruments. We felt this inadequacy especially when we had to carry out difficult urethroplastic operations. However," the report added, "gratitude is due to the Congolese nurses in that they were very interested in their profession, and were happy to acquire more knowledge and learn new surgical methods."

A Congolese Red Cross worker gives out food

Congolese nurses and medical assistants almost everywhere proved excellent. Many foreign nurses were therefore released at the end of the three-month period for which they had volunteered. In most cases the Red Cross doctors were asked to remain longer. Many agreed to do so. Other volunteers arrived to take the place of those who had to leave. Eventually all the volunteers would be replaced by doctors the WHO was recruiting to serve in the Congo on a long-term basis, or by the Congolese doctors already being trained by the WHO. But in the meantime the Congo depended on the Red Cross program, which eventually brought into the country a total of fifty-seven medical teams from twenty-three lands.

At the same time, too, hospital equipment was being improved by Red Cross gifts. ICRC and League delegates, making regular visits to the various teams, always took along drugs, serums, dressings and surgical instruments. After a time the Red Cross was also able to furnish a technician who went from hospital to hospital repairing damaged x-ray equipment.

But the best medicines and equipment could not wipe out illnesses caused by inadequate food, by contaminated water or by disease-carrying insects. And they were the most frequent problems the doctors had to face.

"The nutritional state of the population is catastrophic," an Austrian team reported. "Many of the patients explained that only every third or fourth day did they get anything to eat. Thus we found a five-year-old child weighing only fifteen pounds, or a fifty-year-old woman, five feet tall, weighing fifty pounds."

"More than half of the in-patients were treated for malaria," a Pakistan team reported. A Venezuelan team also found mosquito-transmitted malaria one of the two diseases it had to treat most frequently; the other was bilharziasis, a disease transmitted by fresh-water snails.

The Red Cross doctors thus often spent their scant spare time inspecting water sources and encouraging mosquito-control spraying programs. They worked with WHO experts to improve the nutritional level in the country. They started classes in disease-prevention for patients and for their own Congolese staff.

Certain Congolese customs made the foreigners' difficult task even more difficult.

"The patients wander in and out at will and often go home for the night or otherwise disappear," one Canadian team reported from a hospital in Gemena, close to the equator. "If they are too ill to go home, the whole family moves in, the children sleeping on the bed and the wife under the bed. All the patients are supplied with food by their families, who either cook right on the balconies or in the wards, or on the ground a few yards away."

A Danish lawyer—a man who had already worked with the Red Cross relief program for Hungarian refugees in Austria, and for Algerian refugees in Morocco—was the League's chief delegate in the Congo. Like the ICRC delegates, he visited teams in their hospitals as often as possible. Usually he traveled by plane, because few roads had been built through the country's wild jungles and empty savannahs. When he heard that an earthquake had damaged a hospital in Uvira, on the shores of Lake Tanganyika, he flew more than 1,000 miles and walked for the good part of a day in order to check on the safety of the Swedish team working there.

He found the doctor and the two nurses alive and able to smile over the experience by then. The hospital had rocked perilously. The doctor and his staff, carrying patients to the comparative safety of the yard outside, had been unable to prevent some from jumping through the windows in their fright.

"I was scared to death myself," the Swedish doctor admitted. Then he added, with a grin, that for two weeks afterward, because his patients refused to go back into the hospital, he was forced to operate on them under a magnolia tree. Often he worked with only one hand; he needed the other to brush away flies.

The Danish delegate had his own crisis. Once, arriving at a tiny jungle airport, he found himself facing a party of Congolese armed with machine guns and poisoned arrows. They could be convinced of the peacefulness of his purpose only after hours of talk.

On another occasion, when many doctors were arriving at once in the capital city of Léopoldville, he found accommodations for the members of a German Democratic Republic team in one big room at a mission. Late that same night a medical team came in from the German Federal Republic, and had to be assigned beds in the same large room.

Teams from East and West Germany had not previously worked together on a Red Cross program. The delegate hurried to the mission early the next morning, hoping that their political differences had not caused an open quarrel. His worries proved groundless. The two teams were happily breakfasting together, deep in a discussion of Congo medical conditions.

A formal report issued later by the ICRC and the League called attention to that kind of co-operation. In the Congo, the report said, Red Cross personnel from all six continents had pooled their efforts for the first time, "with teams from Africa, Asia, Oceania and South America working side by side with teams from Europe and North America."

There were outstanding heroes among the Red Cross volunteers in the Congo.

There was the Yugoslav doctor who stayed at his post in Bukava for nine months, often under fire, often keeping two hospitals going although it meant operating steadily for fourteen hours a day.

There was the Irish doctor who remained alone for almost

a year in the small town of Beni, looking after his patients there even after he himself was stricken by one of their tropical diseases.

There was the Belgian woman and the two men, one Dutch and one Swiss, who gave their lives trying to help others in the name of the Red Cross.

The Swiss, Georges Olivet, was a young man who had been living and working in the Congo for some years. He had a successful business. He was widely known among the Congolese, and looked upon as their friend. He could almost certainly have kept his office open, and his business active, even during the disturbances. Instead, as many other Swiss in other parts of the world had done before him, he simply took it for granted that in such circumstances he should devote all his time and energy to the Red Cross.

On the very day the ICRC delegate first arrived in the Congo, therefore, Olivet officially closed his office and offered the delegate the use of its space and equipment. Olivet also made himself and his car available to the delegate on a round-the-clock basis.

Matter-of-fact and efficient, Olivet took on any job that needed doing, whether it was typing lists of hospital equipment or introducing the delegate to the head of the Congo state. Because the Congolese trusted Olivet, they listened when he talked to them. Because he trusted them, he never hesitated to undertake a mission even in an area all other Europeans had deserted.

He helped transport supplies deep into the jungle, and worked for hours in the steamy heat until everything was safely unloaded and distributed. He drove a Red Cross ambulance through the streets of Elisabethville, when Katanga and UN forces were fighting there, in order to pick up the wounded and take them to the shelter of a hospital.

After a year and a half of such service he set out in an ambulance one day to try to reach UN headquarters. His

Georges Olivet distributing supplies

purpose was to bring about a truce that would permit the evacuation of civilians from Elisabethville. With Olivet were Madame Nicole Vroonen of Belgium and Styts Smeding of the Netherlands, both living in Katanga at the time and both members of the Katanga Red Cross.

Military guards stopped the ambulance and turned it back. Olivet tried again. Once more he was unable to get through the lines. A third time he and his two companions made the attempt.

They never reached their destination. Three days later their bullet-riddled ambulance was found empty at the side of the road. Their bodies were eventually discovered nearby, in hastily dug graves.

For a century the sign of the red cross, painted on that ambulance, had moved men to great tasks of service for the suffering and the needy; for a century it had symbolized the only great idea in the world's history in whose name no man had ever killed a fellow man. Yet at the end of that hundred years those who dared to live by the principles of the Red Cross could still sometimes pay for their courage with their lives.

News of that useless tragedy in the Congo flooded the Geneva offices of the International Committee with telegrams from all over the world. Many of those messages of shock and grief were printed in the next issue of the monthly *International Review of the Red Cross*. There was not room for all of them. The *Review* was too crowded with reports of other recent events and current Red Cross activities.

That January, 1962, issue contained, among other items, a statement that the ICRC had just received from the Secretary-General of the UN, confirming the UN's insistence on its armed forces' applying the principles of the Geneva Conventions "as scrupulously as possible."

Here is a sampling of some of the other subjects mentioned in that issue:

ICRC missions to Algeria and Laos, two areas where fighting was then going on; at both places Red Cross delegates had visited prisoners and supervised the distribution of Red Cross relief supplies.

The consignment of a relief shipment of concentrated food to the Togolese Red Cross, to help in its program on behalf of refugees who had recently settled in Togo.

The new responsibilities assumed by the Indonesian Red Cross which had been entrusted with the task of aiding the Netherlands subjects remaining in Indonesia after the end of Dutch rule there.

A conference on radiation medicine, called by the Red

Cross of the German Federal Republic, and attended by an ICRC delegate.

The work still being done in the Central Tracing Agency, sixteen years after the end of World War II, "to identify interned Italian military personnel in German hands who died in captivity in Germany or in German-occupied territory"; in that one section of the Agency alone 400 cases were being handled each month.

The work of the Nicaraguan Red Cross during recent troubles in that country; the president of the Society had reported that "as soon as our Society learned that a group of revolutionaries had invaded Nicaraguan territory and that the National Guard was making preparations for defense, it offered its services . . ."

And, as part of a long report on the work being done by the International Red Cross in the Congo, there was a statement about the founding of a new Congolese Red Cross. Many of its members, under Belgian rule, had belonged to the Congo section of the Belgian National Society; now, like the people of many new African nations, they were preparing to take their own place in the long roll of National Red Cross (and Red Crescent and Red Lion and Sun) Societies. By 1962 there were nearly ninety of them, and the number was still growing.

There was already a Junior Red Cross in the Congo. An ICRC delegate wrote that its members "performed magnificent work at the beginning of July in connection with the wholesale evacuation of European civilians. In August they resumed and extended the milk and vitamin distribution in the main districts of Léopoldville, which was made possible by an initial gift from the ICRC, followed by regular donations from the emergency supply service of UNICEF." By acting as interpreters and intermediaries for ICRC delegates, the Juniors gave further "invaluable service," an official report said.

In a land whose first native doctors were still being trained, those young people could see more than empty words in the universal Red Cross program of "Health through education, and education through health."

In a land brought to bloodshed by bitter hatreds, they could understand why Red Cross Juniors throughout the world were pledging themselves to destroy the ignorance and the prejudices that breed hate, and to break down the barriers separating people of different races, different colors, different creeds.

Their own new Congo organization, coming into being at a time when the Red Cross was a century old, was proof in itself that the Red Cross was not static.

Congolese Juniors are pledged to destroy racial prejudices

It never has been static. Created out of war, it has endured many conflicts. It has grown as the demands upon it grew; it has changed as times have changed. It is still growing and still changing.

Only the principles for which it stands, however often they are ignored, remain unchanged and speak now as in the past for the conscience of the world.

To relieve suffering wherever it exists, to see the human being in every enemy, to prove that humanity can survive even in the midst of inhumanity—these are the ideals Henry Dunant first put into words. Today those words unite 130 million people in a brotherhood unique in man's history.

Perhaps before another century has ended that brotherhood will be extended into every corner of the earth, and every man will look at his fellow men and say, as Dunant heard those women say at Castiglione, "All are brothers!"

FOR FURTHER READING

A Suggested List of Books

BARTON, CLARA: *The Red Cross in Peace and War.* Washington, D.C.: American Historical Press, 1889.

BARTON, CLARA: *A Story of the Red Cross.* New York: D. Appleton & Co., 1904.

BICKNELL, ERNEST P.: *Pioneering with the Red Cross.* New York: The Macmillan Company, 1935.

COURSIER, HENRI: *The International Red Cross.* Geneva: 1961. (Translated from the French, *La Croix-rouge internationale.* Paris: Presses universitaires de France, 1959.)

DULLES, FOSTER RHEA: *The American Red Cross—A History.* New York: Harper & Brothers, 1950.

DUNANT, HENRY: *A Memory of Solferino.* Washington, D.C.: The American Red Cross, 1959. (Translated from the French, *Un souvenir de Solferino,* 1862.)

Geneva Conventions of 1949, The. Geneva: ICRC, 1949.

GUMPERT, MARTIN: *The Story of the Red Cross.* New York: Oxford University Press, 1938.

HURD, CHARLES W.: *Compact History of the American Red Cross.* New York: Hawthorn Books, Inc., 1959.

JOYCE, JAMES AVERY: *The Red Cross International and the Strategy of Peace.* New York: Oceana Publications, Inc., 1959.

KERNODLE, P. B.: *The Red Cross Nurse in Action*. New York: Harper & Brothers, 1949.

KORSON, GEORGE: *At His Side*. New York: Coward-McCann, Inc., 1945.

MALONY, JOHN: *Let There Be Mercy*. New York: Doubleday, Doran & Company, Inc. 1941.

PICTET, JEAN S.: *The Red Cross Principles;* with a Preface by Max Huber. Geneva: ICRC, 1956.

ROSS, ISHBEL: *Angel of the Battlefield: The Life of Clara Barton*. New York: Harper & Brothers, 1956.

Index

Index